DATE DUE

OE 21 02			

DEMCO 38-296

REDISCOVERING

VALUES

REDISCOVERING

VALUES

Coming to Terms
with Postmodernism

Hugh Mercer Curtler

M.E. Sharpe
Armonk, New York
London, England

Library of Congress Cataloging-in-Publication Data

Curtler, Hugh Mercer.
Rediscovering values : coming to terms with Postmodernism /
Hugh M. Curtler.
p. cm.
Includes bibliographical references and index.
ISBN 0-7656-0059-5 (alk. paper).
1. Postmodernism (Literature)   2. Values in literature.
I. Title.
PN98.P67C88   1997
801'.3—dc21   97-9281
CIP
Printed in the United States of America

EB (c)   10   9   8   7   6   5   4   3   2

To my sons:

Hugh and Rudy

Contents

Acknowledgments

This book started out to be a collection of essays written on the subject of values during the past thirty years. Two things quickly became evident: (1) several of the essays were outdated and the collection lacked coherence as a result, and (2) my increasing interest in the postmodern attack on values in recent years could easily provide a frame of reference to help make the collection coherent. This necessitated rewriting several of the essays, writing three new chapters, and combining parts of several separate essays into one new chapter.

I want to thank *Modern Age* for allowing me to reprint, albeit in this peculiar fashion, several essays that appeared in that journal over the years. That periodical is where I first introduced the notion of "inverted consciousness" in the summer of 1985. I should also like to thank *Conradiana* for permission to print a portion of my essay defending Conrad from Chinua Achebe's libel that he was a racist and, therefore, *Heart of Darkness* cannot be considered a great novel. That essay began my inquiries into the concept of "greatness" in literature and expanded into the present sixth chapter. The seventh chapter is a revision of a paper that first appeared in *Forum for Honors,* published by the National Collegiate Honors Society in 1994 as "Citizenship in a World of Difference." It has been greatly expanded.

Several people played instrumental roles in the process of bringing this book to light. To begin with, Peter Coveney at M.E. Sharpe encouraged me to start the project. Of inestimable help was Wally Beasley, my colleague and friend in faraway Georgia, who showed infinite patience and vision in helping to transform heterogeneous essays into a coherent whole. A former student and friend, Kevin Stroup, read an early version of the manuscript, gave me encouragement, and reassured me that the book wasn't overly narrow or technical. Connie McQuillen and Marianne Zarzana echoed that reassurance, and Marianne edited several key chapters in order to enable me to make my ideas clearer. Finally, my colleague Stewart Day made a number of helpful comments on an early version of the second chapter.

I would like to blame these people for the book's failings, but alas, I cannot. The blame is mine alone.

Cottonwood, Minnesota
December 1996

REDISCOVERING

VALUES

Introduction

We live in troubling times. But like Mrs. Jellyby, her head filled with notions of Borrioboola-Gha, we bluster effusively over trivia while all around us serious problems go unattended. "Conservatives" (who don't give a moment's thought to conservation) worry about the gross national product and interest rates, while "liberals" tinker with a broken social machine and busily add names to the list of society's victims. Environmentalists make impossible demands as their critics holler about "jobs" while downsizing. Nations that are able to do so stockpile nuclear weapons, while those that aren't try to find out how to join the fray; terrorists and political dissidents stand by to pick up the scraps. While we complain about maintaining our "quality of life," we can hear the politicians in the background dickering about where to put the growing tonnage of nuclear waste that we produce. Overhead the ozone thins while we cut down rain forests, plan a new golf course in Las Vegas, and take little note of our diminishing aquifers, global warming, and desertification. Human populations increase exponentially as resources disappear. In the meantime, we send out for pizza, get a cold one out of the fridge, and make plans to attend the latest action flick.

We quibble about the seriousness of these problems and split hairs about the accuracy of the predictions, forgetting that even if these bleak predictions are wrong, prudence requires that we err on the side of caution. However, we cannot get the attention of policy makers, who have small minds and narrow vision and worry only about the latest poll and re-election next year.

In the midst of the din, a few shrill voices decry the decline of "family values." The terms are not defined, but these people seem worried about the demise of the "nuclear family" and increasing violence in the streets, while strident young men and women on the other side of the political fence seek only to "level the playing field," remove the "glass ceiling," and reduce the "gender gap."

Ironically, the major problem we confront as a species is not on the list I have just enumerated. Nor does it lie in the fact that these problems tend to compound one another. Our main problem is that we refuse to admit that we have serious problems: we happily delude ourselves into thinking that these issues are mere fictions. We are witnessing group denial on a scale of mammoth proportions.

Accounting for our refusal to deal with critical issues is difficult, but Aldous Huxley was certainly correct in noting in the early 1930s how susceptible we are to mindless diversions. Quite possibly, our refusal stems from fear of the unknown and uncertainty about the future, which translate into the delusion that technology will solve all our problems. Clearly, we feel cut off from one another and from a world of sense and meaning: we are experiencing a crisis of spirit that translates into a preoccupation with ourselves and our immediate creature comforts. We suffer from what I call "inverted consciousness," which exhibits itself in our unwillingness, or inability, to confront one another as persons and to acknowledge our responsibility to preserve the world we share.

The phenomenon of inverted consciousness reveals itself in a diminished sense of the Other coupled with a growing sense of our own importance. The subject makes of himself or herself the object of consciousness, and the world (and other persons) is seen as merely an extension of the self: they exist for us merely as a source of pleasure or pain. Humans have always been motivated by self-interest, and a concern with the self is not only "normal" but also legitimate. When consciousness becomes inverted, however, self-interest becomes self-absorption. A legitimate concern for individuality, rights, and personal autonomy has degenerated into individual*ism,* "a war of all against all, the pursuit of happiness to the dead end of narcissistic preoccupation with the self" (Lasch 1991, xv). The evidence that this has occurred surrounds us. The symbol of our times is the Sony Walkman, attached jockeylike to the head of a middle-aged man (or woman) jogging to maintain a youthful appearance, with glazed eyes, totally unaware of what surrounds him as he hears only his own breathing and the sounds inside his head.

One of the major losses from this inversion of consciousness is our awareness of value: we simply do not look at and listen to what occurs around us, and we are becoming increasingly blind and deaf. The price we pay is a shrinking world and a refusal to attend to the problems that need attention until they force their way into the innermost circle of our consciousness and become a problem for us, here and now. Even then, we cry, "Not in my backyard!" as we try to push the problems away and foist them on someone else. Unfortunately, buck-passing and crisis management will not suffice: some of the problems we face cannot wait much longer to be solved.

In this book, I argue for a clearer understanding of the nature of values, which I am convinced surround us. We must rediscover them, because we ignore them at great cost. This is not a defense of "family values" (whatever those might be) but a plea to reorient our thinking, turn our attention away from ourselves, and wake up to the world and Others that surround and sustain us, and at times threaten us as well.

On a more mundane level, however, the person on the street is convinced that values are not real, they do not exist "out there" in the world. Values are nothing more than feelings, and they vary from person to person and with time and place. That is, they, too, are merely extensions of the self. This conviction, which is seldom questioned, is one of the major symptoms of our inverted consciousness, and it is mistaken. I attempt to draw attention to this mistake and the various forms it has taken, and I suggest an alternative way to regard values themselves. My focus, for the most part, is upon the problems as they have surfaced in the academy. But the implications of my argument go beyond the walls of academe to raise questions about the legitimacy of such concerns as "political correctness" and the "cult of the victim."

I focus on the academy because that is where I am most at home and because education can provide the tourniquet we must apply if we hope to stop the bleeding from self-inflicted wounds. Unfortunately, educators are also preoccupied with trivialities and refuse to examine such basic issues as the purpose of higher education, which is utterly confused at present.

Within the academy in recent years, the specter of "postmodernism" has appeared and gained considerable strength. This movement began in France among a handful of intellectuals who shared a desire to "deconstruct" texts and read them anew in order to find hidden meanings. It has degenerated, in this country, into a form of nihilism that rejects out of hand the reality of the "text" in the student's hand (which is the *reductio ad absurdum* of inverted consciousness, surely) and any sort of evaluation about what makes texts "great." In its extreme form, the movement is intolerant and somewhat incoherent; in moderation, it seeks only to direct attention away from "privileged" perspectives, which is a worthy goal.

To someone reading this book whose only contact with the academic community comes from having done time there, the question might arise, Why be concerned about postmodernism and silly disputes among academics about traditional ways of learning? The answer is, of course, that ideas have a way of making an impact upon the "real" world. Indeed, the nihilistic tendencies within postmodernism have already begun to make themselves felt outside the ivory tower. Consider, for example, the militant factions advancing revisionist history within high school curricula, not to mention the growing number of avant-garde architects who insist that buildings can be constructed without knowing anything about materials or the laws of physics. Recall, also, that today's students are tomorrow's leaders. Furthermore, postmodern thinking has fostered what is popularly referred to as "political correctness" and has initiated widespread alarm on behalf of the victims of social injustice—real or imagined. Like so much postmodern thought, these popular spin-offs begin with important insights—such as the role of interpretation in the writing of history, the tendency of language and conventional preconceptions to entrap our minds, and the need for sensitivity to human suffering. Unfortunately, many of these thinkers push these insights beyond reasonable conclusions. Thus, for example, what begins with Nietzsche as a legitimate concern for the hegemonic tendencies inherent in knowledge claims passes through Michel Foucault's passionate concern for the abuses of power and results in such absurdities as the prohibition against advertising the exceptional view of a home on the beach because it might offend the visually impaired.

In a word, postmodernism is not a movement confined to a small group of radicals behind ivy-covered walls who want to trash Western tradition. Admittedly, some of the disputes are silly, but the movement as a whole has broad ramifications that affect us all and demands a closer look.

I would insist, however, that postmodernism is not the enemy. The enemy is the relativism, exclusivity, reductionism, hyperbole, and half-truth that dwell in the heart of the beast. Postmodernism is merely one symptom among many that leads to a bleak prognosis for the future of humankind if, indeed, education is our great hope. Thus, since one must begin somewhere, my call to rediscover values will concern itself with the growing influence of postmodernism with an eye toward restoring some sense of balance in our thinking and redirecting attention to problems that require solutions. The central issue that confronts us in this book, then, is whether or not values are *real* or whether we have nothing better to talk about than ourselves.

The point was well made by Cervantes in what I regard as a parable for our times.

> "[T]ell me," [queried Sancho,] "by what you love best, is this Ciudad Real wine?"
>
> "Oh rare wine taster!" said he of the Grove; "nowhere else indeed does it come from, and it has some years' age, too."
>
> "Leave me alone for that," said Sancho; "never fear but I'll hit upon the place it came from somehow. What would you say, sir squire, to my having such a great natural instinct in judging wines that you only have to let me smell one and I can tell positively its country, its kind, its flavor and soundness, the changes it will undergo, and everything that appertains to a wine? But it's no wonder, for I have had in my family, on my father's side, the two best wine-tasters that have been known in La Mancha for many a long year, and to prove it I'll tell you now a thing that happened to them. They gave the two of them some wine out of a cask, to try, asking their opinion as to the condition, quality, goodness, or badness of the wine. One of them tried it with the tip of his tongue, the other did no more than bring it to his nose. The first said the wine had a flavor of iron, the second said it had a stronger flavor of cordovan leather. The owner said the cask was clean, and that nothing had been added to the wine from which it could have

got a flavor of either iron or leather. Nevertheless, these two great wine-tasters held to what they had said, and when the time came to clean the cask, they found in it a small key hanging to a thong of cordovan leather; see now if one who comes from the same stock does not have a right to give his opinion in such cases."

—Cervantes, *Don Quixote* (II, 13)

One of the many things a parable such as this teaches us is that, in order to make sensible judgments about wine, we must acquire a discerning taste. Not all wines are the same. Similarly, judgments of value require discriminating taste and should not be dismissed summarily by those who consider them silly or unfounded. We must open ourselves to the possibility that there may be a key in the cask tied to a leather thong.

Chapter 1

Inverted Consciousness
and the Eclipse of Values

*Pluralism is not relativism. It does not mean the
denial of absolutes or the absence of standards.*
—A. Bartlett Giamatti

Culture may have arisen thousands of years ago when
members of the species *Homo sapiens* paused in their fren-
zied attempt to catch wild game and saw, for the first time,
the beauty of an animal in flight. Or it arose when other
members of the same genus huddled in fear and imagined
the angry face of their tormentor hurling mighty thunder-
bolts from the heavens. We don't really know. What we do
know is that, eons ago, primitive humans suddenly needed
to communicate their feelings with more than grunts and
gestures. They began with painting. Then, written language
slowly evolved from the tangle of confused images and
sounds as these early humans struggled to explain what

disturbed them deeply. As understanding grew, and they began to feel more comfortable among the members of the tribe, and later the community, they developed philosophy and science to systematize the world into parts and categories. Thus, with the growth in size of communities came civilization, and at the center of civilization lay culture in the form of art and myth, religion, language, and science.[1] Ortega has said that civilization is above all else the will to live in common. If this is so, then culture is the expression in human terms of our shared experience of a common world.

Culture provides members of human communities with a set of lenses through which they come to see their world. That vision is clearest when the civilization that houses it is healthiest—that is, as Toynbee noted, when it is most creative and energetic. When civilizations lose their creativity and energy, however, the problems that confront them become overwhelming, and solutions are not at hand: a period of breakdown and disintegration begins. At such times, the lenses through which people look at their world cloud over, and that world becomes blurred.

Though Toynbee hesitated to say so fifty years ago when he wrote *A Study of History,* Western civilization has entered into such a period of breakdown and disintegration. More to the point, high culture, which has evolved over many centuries and survived a number of diverse civilizations, is under siege from various quarters; it is being transmogrified from an articulate and coherent expression of immensely rich and varied human experience into one shrill voice among many clamoring for an audience. We are witnessing the devolution of high culture into cultural pluralism.

The new sets of cultural lenses through which we view our world—and we are admonished not to insist that one set is superior to another—reveal a world that is fractured and incoherent. Art is becoming increasingly personal and narcissistic; religion has been replaced by therapy; language has become impoverished; and cognition stagnates at the level of personal opinion. What is happening?

⁓

The cultural crisis that confronts us can be understood only by examining the threads that have held high culture together and that began to fray as a result of the Enlightenment, the Protestant Reformation, and the scientific and industrial revolutions. If we are to understand our present crisis, we must begin by examining its sources. What began in optimism and hope has turned into a schism within the human soul born of disillusionment.

No age or movement is born *ex nihilo*. We can trace the origins of the period twentieth-century historians call the Age of Enlightenment back through Descartes to Galileo. Despite a weak romantic undertow fostered in prior centuries by people like Montaigne and Pascal, together with the ineffective "Storm and Stress" movement in Germany, the eighteenth century was, in the West, intoxicated with reason and the scientific method. It was a fascination that began with mathematics and astronomy and exploded into an industrial revolution that has affected the entire planet. The compulsion to quantify and the narrowing of focus upon short-run solutions to the problems at hand have generated a technological imperative that propels us in the name of "progress" toward an increasingly uncertain future.

This idolatry of reason generated boundless optimism as modern thinkers worshiped at the shrine of their own methods and inventions; displacement of the immense authority of the Catholic church was required, and the attack occurred on various fronts. The Puritans, following thinkers such as John Calvin, led the attack—especially in sixteenth- and seventeenth-century England—advancing laissez-faire capitalism, which ate away at the foundations and authority of the Church until its influence upon Western society was no more. "Surprise has sometimes been expressed that the Church should not have been more effective in giving inspiration and guidance during the immense economic reorganization to which tradition has assigned the not very felicitous name 'The Industrial Revolution.' It did not give it, because it did not possess it" (Tawney 1962, 193).

The problem is, as Dostoyevsky knew so clearly, the human spirit at all times and in all places requires miracle and mystery, and human beings flounder and grope without spiritual authority and sustaining myths. For all its excesses, the Catholic church gave to Europeans during the Dark Ages a sense of purpose and direction that has steadily disintegrated since the time of the Protestant Reformation. In Jung's words, "one thing is certain: that modern man, Protestant or not, has lost the protection of the ecclesiastical walls carefully erected and reinforced since Roman days, and on account of that loss has approached the zone of world-destroying and world-creating fire. Life has become quickened and intensified. Our world is permeated by waves of restlessness and fear" (Jung 1961, 311).

I do not intend to apologize for the Catholic church, which committed countless atrocities and was thoroughly corrupt at the time of the Protestant Reformation. Nonetheless, the meaning of human existence was clear in prior ages, and it was found through something outside and beyond the self, a Transcendent Being or abiding values. Medieval men and women knew what was good and what was evil. However, their world exhibited a spiritual dimension that could not be quantified and that, therefore, mathematics and the scientific method could not allow.

To be sure, the Enlightenment brought with it a legitimate concern for the rights of persons, a doctrine that has resulted in genuine moral progress in the direction of universal suffrage. Additionally, the scientific revolution generated the industrial revolution, which has brought a higher standard of living to more people than was ever thought possible by Descartes or any of his fellow dreamers. It has also brought us scientific medicine, resulting in longer and healthier lives for ever larger numbers of people. But with these benefits has come an explosion of the human population that threatens our survival. In addition, a legitimate concern for human rights, autonomy, and human individuality has degenerated into an individual*ism* in which all men and women resemble one another. This individualism arose from an increasingly "inverted consciousness," a soul that, as Ortega noted some sixty years ago, has become "hermetically enclosed within itself, incapable of submitting to anything or anybody, believing itself self-sufficient —in a word, indocile" (Ortega 1960, 66).

15

Without God, in a two-dimensional world without value, preoccupied with private aspirations, and with handmade guideposts that do not provide meaningful direction, the human animal gropes and stumbles. The postmodern individual currently experiences what Toynbee called a "sense of drift." More than anything else, perhaps, it is the loss of the spiritual dimension of human experience that has brought about our current malaise. Toynbee asks, in this regard, "Will modern Western man repent of, and recoil from his *hybris* . . . ? The answer cannot yet be forecast, but we may anxiously scan the landscape of our contemporary spiritual life for any symptoms that may give us ground for hope that we are regaining the use of our spiritual faculty which we have been doing our utmost to sterilize" (Toynbee 1963, 455).

Toynbee hesitated to conclude that Western civilization had entered into a period of breakdown and disintegration, because he failed to find evidence of what he called "a counter-resurgence of asceticism." I would suggest that asceticism is present in the form of "inverted consciousness," resulting from an inveterate redirection of attention from object to subject. This phenomenon has evolved from the individualism mentioned above and has, like all forms of asceticism, involved a turning away from the world. For the inverted consciousness, the world is reduced to the world-for-me, and things and persons outside the self are acknowledged only insofar as they are the source of pleasure or pain for a diminished ego.

In the phenomenon of inverted consciousness, the only interesting object for the subject is the subject itself. Since culture is an expression of our common human experience, this inversion of consciousness marks the rejection of culture as such. "Alas," sighed Nietzsche, "the time is coming when man will no longer shoot the arrow of his longing beyond himself, and his bowstring will have forgotten how to whir" (Kaufman 1954, 129).

~

Culture is the word we use to describe common values and the structure and meaning humans have managed to carve out of an otherwise alien and chaotic world. As suggested above, the symbols that are used to inform the matter of experience are provided by myth, religion, language, art, and science. Through these symbolic forms and social institutions, we gradually begin to make sense of a world that would otherwise be silent, hostile, and opaque.

Myth orders and integrates experience that is worked on first by priests, and then by poets and artists, and finally by the philosophers and other "knowers" until it becomes understood. The activity of the poets, in particular, is essential in transforming the brute experience of feeling and imagination into the language that will later be worked over by the philosophers and scientists as they begin to systematize and codify. For example, we no longer see the world the way it was seen before Dante, Shakespeare, and Goethe or as it was before Renoir and Picasso. The world as we now know it is the world as it has been transformed by poets and artists. It behooves us, then, to attend to what the poets and artists have had to say.

Our age has been described variously as an age of anxiety, crisis, and despiritualization; it is an age of alienation in which the privileged ego turns away from the Other and finds itself alone. We exhibit little hope for the future; therefore, "it makes sense to live only for the moment, to fix our eyes on our own 'private performance,' to become connoisseurs of our own decadence, to cultivate 'a transcendental self-attention' " (Lasch 1991, 6). Cut adrift, without moorings, in a world without meaning, where value, it is glibly stated, merely reflects personal affectations, what can an artist or a poet do but engage in "intricate manipulation of subtle features of his medium" (Altieri 1990, 40)? Nothing else occupies his or her attention. "The writer no longer sees life reflected in his own mind. Just the opposite: he sees the world ... as a mirror of himself" (Lasch 1991, 25).

The works of postmodern writers such as Jim Hougan, Tom Wolfe, Peter Marin, Edwin Schur, Paul Zweig, and Richard Sennett reveal the same absorption of the self with itself. Lacking any connection with the world outside and locked in the present moment, the writer journeys into the private self-world and discovers a vacuum: there is nothing important to say because the world revealed there is vapid. In the words of his narrator/hero in *Three Journeys,* Paul Zweig confronts "an experience of inner emptiness, the frightening feeling that at some level of existence I'm nobody, that my identity has collapsed and deep down, no one's there" (Zweig 1976, 149).

The same hollow sound echoes in postmodern drama as works by such writers as Albee, Beckett, Ionesco, and Genet "center on the emptiness, isolation, loneliness, and despair experienced by the borderline personality" (Lasch 1991, 89). Other playwrights, such as Pirandello and

Brecht, try to break down the actor/audience distinction in order to incorporate the audience into the drama. This move does little more than indulge the audience's desire to become pseudoperformers, thereby reinforcing its self-absorption. Attention is directed away from the object and toward the self and its emotional involvement with the action: the play becomes a vehicle for exploring the audience's own emotions and feelings, and little else besides. The spectator, not the play, is the focus of attention.

In the visual arts, postmodern painters, like the poets, find themselves uprooted and trying to create meaning in an absurd universe. Giorgio De Chirico's *The Disquieting Muses,* painted toward the end of the modern era, is typical. It presents a visual mood of inversion, solitude, and separation. It is surely one of the most graphic pictorial statements in an age of dislocation and noisy desperation. The main figure in Chirico's painting stands facing away from the spectator. Another sits with arms folded. They are surreal; they have no faces, no eyes or ears with which to take in the world around them. In the words of Gilles Deleuze and Felix Guattari, they are "bodies without organs" (Deleuze and Guattari 1983, 9). Their attention is directed inward: they are not truly human. Objects are strewn about them in disarray; shadows fall off the canvas to the left. One can see in the distance an empty, hollow city and the suggestion of factory chimneys against a bleak sky. There is no movement whatever; there is no life—with one possible exception. In the shadow toward the right of the canvas, there stands a piece of sculpture holding out one hand tentatively while it covers itself with the other. It appears to be beckoning, a mockery in marble of a human gesture.

19

As we take in the painting, we imagine our ears filled with the sounds of composers like Berg and Schoenberg, echoes of an age that produced atrocities on a scale previously unimaginable, a planet in decay, and a civilization in the process of disintegration. This is an age that, like its art, has no frame of reference; it is an age whose heroes are antiheroes, whose beauty is ugly; it is an age without bearings, beliefs, or solidarity, an age that wallows in solipsism of the present moment, turned in on itself, seeing nothing except as it bears on the *self.*

⌒

The family and the Church are in total disarray. Thus, one turns in desperation to the universities in the hope that the situation is not as grim as it appears. We find, though, that the climate in the universities grows increasingly threatening. To begin with, overspecialization has produced experts whose range of vision is slight and whose use of jargon makes communication impossible with those outside their closed group of disciples. Recall that language is central to culture, which is the attempt to express our common, human experience: overspecialization leads to separatism and isolation. Here and there, one finds small pockets of people willing to attempt the task of preserving the best works of Western culture, in the hope of maintaining a meaningful frame of reference; however, they find it difficult or impossible to pass these works on to an increasingly unwilling student population, whose stunted linguistic skills reduce much of high culture to the level of what Joseph Wood Krutch once called "document."

It is sobering to contemplate the reluctant undergraduate, preoccupied with pleasure and thinking of the future only in terms of job prospects, who approaches the rich tapestry of Shakespeare's language with a working vocabulary of a few thousand words. In response to the diminished vision of both teachers and students, the curricula of the universities have become career-oriented. To make matters worse, preserving high culture has a low priority. Within university departments where bands of guardians once protected Western culture on all fronts, there now reside disciples of black studies, Far Eastern studies, feminism, and devotees of deconstructionism who are convinced that there is no such thing as a "classic" and therefore no culture worth preserving. Concern for the preservation of culture invariably raises the question, "Which culture?" and the specter of what is referred to as "cultural chauvinism."

To insist, as I have, that culture can be found at the center of civilization does not imply that culture and civilization experience the same rhythms of birth, growth, decay, and disintegration. Indeed, as I have suggested above, culture transcends civilization and can endure long after the civilization from which it sprang has decayed and been replaced. Thus it is that "high" culture in the West—which evolved over the centuries from the Greco-Roman, Judeo-Christian, and Germanic civilizations—has managed to survive them all. When I maintain, then, that our present civilization is in retreat, this does not mean that Western culture is *ipso facto* on the decline. Indeed, it may well survive, as it has for centuries, and become a part of the next civilization that arises, phoenixlike, from the ashes of our present one. However, when we confront the linguistic paralysis, the spiritual vacuum in contemporary human experience, the widespread ignorance of science and philosophy, and the absence of new myths to replace the old, we must pause.

Given the present movement toward a plurality of cultures (which is inexorable), one can expect that remnants of traditional, high culture will survive, but only in a bewildering mix. In American universities and colleges, for example, "humanities" courses will doubtless continue to struggle with more "practical" courses for a place in the curriculum: they will be increasingly on the defensive, as they seek to accommodate a largely illiterate, immature, and preoccupied audience. The material will be selected according to egalitarian principles along ideological lines, being certain to include "representative" works authored by persons of color, women, and non-Western cultures. There will be a diminishing number of works from traditional Western culture, and the works that are selected will doubtless be in the form of excerpts with notes of explanation in italics. In this plethora of cultures, none will be any better or worse than any other; none will be "high," and none will be "low." They will simply be *different*.

This process will not result simply in cultural diversity—which is an appealing notion in many ways—but in a leveling down of high culture to the mundane. High culture will have become "commodified" culture: the butterfly will have metamorphosed into a caterpillar.[2]

A consciousness that is inverted, restricted to its own

narrow field of vision and thereby limited to the range of its own feelings and moods, cannot produce dimensions of universality in works of art and literature. Both will therefore lack what Jung called "vision" and become increasingly personal. Individual differences will be glorified at the expense of shared human experience. As noted above, this trend has already begun.

Today, we find ourselves surrounded by intellectuals who cannot distinguish sentiment from sentimentality, truth from opinion, or fact from fiction. Personal anecdote passes for historical insight, and sincerity is the only measure of true genius. Since many of these people "teach" in institutions of "higher education," the situation can only become worse. Harold Bloom thinks that when the present "chaotic age" is over and a new "theocratic age" dawns, the English departments in those institutions will be reduced to the present size of the classics departments—and I would add, the latter will have disappeared. Departments in the social sciences and humanities will be peopled by crypto-anthropologists and sociologists posing as philosophers or historians, whose disciplines will be impossible to distinguish from one another. If this were simply a move away from specialization, one might well celebrate. But unfortunately, it is a reductionistic move that casts aside important methodological differences between the disciplines that are their only rationale. As I shall show in the next chapter, such reductionism stems from the current rejection of "the despised logos." Surely, William Inge was right when he said, "Ancient civilizations were destroyed by imported barbarians; we have bred our own" (Inge 1920, 13). More to the point, we have given them rank and tenure.

If we can come to fully understand these forces, perhaps we can resist them and alter their future course. This would appear to be the import of what historians of culture have come to call the "postmodern" movement, except for those members of the movement who have given up on human-kind altogether. In this regard, a great many postmodern thinkers would agree with much of my assessment of our current malaise. They would insist, though, that the signs of decay I have noted are signs of the death throes of modern-ism and that a new, postmodern, age is dawning in which the human spirit will be reborn. I shall examine this theme in the next chapter. For the moment, I would simply note that the difficulty with postmodernism is that it would bury what is vital along with what is dead in Western culture. In spite of my own concerns over the mistakes we have made in the name of "modernism," I would argue that if we are to deal successfully with the forces our civilization has unleashed, we cannot survive without preserving what is best from our past.

Some readers will doubtless argue that the view I am pre-senting here is merely a reflection of what Richard Hofstad-ter called a "paranoid style" that involves belief in "a conspiracy directed against . . . culture." As a result, I am simply one of those reactionary conservatives who "sees the fate of this conspiracy in apocalyptic terms . . . always manning the barricades of civilization" (Hofstadter 1965, 40). I hope this is not the case, but even if it is, one might be well advised to listen, because paranoia may be symp-tomatic of a deeper awareness.

However, in order to show that my concerns do not merely stem from a sense of nostalgia over a golden age that has now passed, I will admit to doubting that such an age ever existed. I do not number myself among those whom Lawrence Levine insists are "jeremiads" who think the sky is falling and have no historical sense of the present struggle. Further, in order to dispel the notion that my concerns stem from my paranoia, I should add that I see no conspiracy anywhere; what I see is confusion, increasing intolerance, and inverted consciousness.

At times, I share Harold Bloom's pessimism in light of the inroads already made by what he calls "the school of Resentment." At other times, I cling to the hope that sanguine thinkers such as Lawrence Levine are right and that the profound changes we are going through will not be permanent and that some good will come of them. After all, cultural diversity is, in itself, a worthy and lofty goal whose time is long overdue. Additionally, modernism has too long ignored the human spirit, as I noted at the outset of this chapter. What we must beware, however, is the tendency to join forces with those who would revolt against a tradition that, albeit flawed, is nevertheless extraordinary. We must work our way carefully through the criticisms and acknowledge those that are germane and reject those that are bogus or inflated. I began this task in the last section, but there is considerable work to be done.

My suggestion is that we begin with a careful assessment of the postmodern challenge and then determine whether we can stem the tide of resentment characterized above. If my analysis of the problem is correct, we can do this only by preserving what is vital from a rapidly vanishing past, avoiding the temptations of reduction and half-truth, and by redirecting attention away from the self and toward the world. In a word, we must rescue the concept of "greatness" from the demystifiers of postmodernism and re-establish the centrality of values to discussions about our common world.

Notes

1. This account is a somewhat simplified attempt to combine views expressed by both Eliseo Vivas and Ernst Cassirer. See, for example, Ernst Cassirer, *Language and Myth,* translated by Susanne Langer (New York: Dover Publications, 1946), especially ch. 1; and Eliseo Vivas, *The Artistic Transaction* (Columbus: Ohio State University Press, 1963), 3–30.

2. The expression "commodified culture" is that of Robert Heilbroner, *The Nature and Logic of Capitalism* (New York: Norton, 1985), 140. Heilbroner describes "commodified culture" as "the cacophony of ten thousand books, magazines, and television impressions . . . in the end a recipe for confusion rather than enlightenment."

Chapter 2

The Postmodern Challenge

*[T]he project of modernity (the realization of
universality) has not been forsaken or forgotten, but
destroyed, "liquidated." . . . "Auschwitz" can be
taken as a paradigmatic name for the tragic
"incompletion" of modernity.*

—Jean-François Lyotard

The modern epoch began with Galileo and Descartes in the
seventeenth century and according to Jean-François
Lyotard, who coined the term *postmodern,* ended with
Auschwitz. I shall reserve comment on this point for later.
Modernism is characterized, as noted in the last chapter, by
a deep commitment to reason and the methods of the physi-
cal sciences whereby humans could (as Descartes put it)
"make [themselves] masters and possessors of nature." It is
also characterized by the dwindling influence of the Church
and the relegation of articles of faith to the waste heap of
superstition. In its wake have come concerns for the rights
of men and women, scientific medicine, the industrial revo-

lution, technological advances to fascinate and boggle the mind, and environmental destruction on a grand scale.

"Postmodernism" is a reaction to modernism and to anything that smacks of reason, science, "progress," or the Enlightenment. It began in Europe with a group of French intellectuals who sought answers to some of the perplexing philosophical difficulties they inherited from German idealism.

One of the major components of postmodernism—deconstructionism—began with Jacques Derrida's reading and rereading of Hegel and Heidegger and the latter's attempt to rethink the problem of being and becoming as Parmenides and other pre-Socratics misconstrued it. Derrida, a trained philosopher, wanted to direct the attention of other philosophers to the plurality of possible readings of philosophical texts. Most mainstream philosophers in England and the United States have ignored the movement, though thinkers such as Richard Rorty have attempted to water it down and turn it into a weakened form of pragmatism that reduces truth to "North Atlantic bourgeois liberalism" (Norris 1987, 157). The major impact of deconstructionist and other poststructuralist thinkers such as Derrida has been in literary criticism, where it has been turned into a thin stew made up of pop psychology, sociology, and anthropology by people who, with the exception of a few thinkers like Rorty and Allan Megill, have little philosophical training. In their attempt to move heavy metaphysical buckets that were imported from ancient Greece to Germany and then on to France, they exhibit neither the will nor the strength, and the results are disappointing, for the most part. In sum, what started as a problem in ontology—namely, the joining together of science, morality, art, and religion, which Kant had rent asunder—was quickly transformed in this country into a nontheory of literature by literary critics who, for the most part, have little interest in problems of ontology or the subtleties of German idealism.

It is difficult to characterize such a heterogeneous group of thinkers who agree about little except that the modern era is over and that the postmodern must begin with emphasis on intuition, everyday life, local knowledge, specifics, the contingent, personal testimony, and direct experience rather than theory and abstractions. Their enemy is what Calvin Schrag has aptly termed "the despised logos" (Schrag 1992, 17ff.). On the whole, postmodernism "appropriates, transforms, and transcends French structuralism, romanticism, phenomenology, nihilism, populism, existentialism, hermeneutics, Western Marxism, critical theory, and anarchism" (Rosenau 1992, 13). As a movement, it is "distressingly noodle-like. . . . If one looks for a common sense of beliefs or doctrines that bind the thought of the various contributors, one is again informed, and certainly with considerable evidence, that postmodernism is neither a theory nor a platform of doctrines. . . . Pinning down a referent of 'postmodernism' is indeed very much like pinning down a drop of mercury" (Schrag 1992, 6).

In fact, these thinkers tend to agree more about what they reject than about what they accept. At the same time, however, there are some prominent themes that tend to recur in their writings. One can also make out two rather different camps within the parameters of postmodernism, roughly separated by geography and nationality. The more extreme camp is made up of such thinkers as Derrida, Michel Foucault, J. Baudrillard, Gilles Deleuze, Jean-François Lyotard, Alain Touraine, John Laffey, Fernand Braudel, and Gianni Vattimo. Motivated for the most part by an impending sense of the "end of history" (Baudrillard) and a concern for the plight of the disempowered, these European thinkers tend to be nihilistic. As a group, they tend to encourage an attitude of "incredulity toward metanarratives"; they would refine our "sensitivity to differences," insist that we "tolerate the incommensurables," and arm ourselves for "a war on totality" (Lyotard 1992, xxiv, xxv, 82).

The European arm of this movement is to be distinguished from its American followers, made up largely of literary critics, historians, and social scientists who tend to be proactive and committed to a variety of political causes. This group consists of such thinkers as Ben Agger, Allan Megill, Manfred Frank, Fred Dallmayr, Julia Kristeva, Anthony Giddens, David Griffin, Barbara Herrnstein Smith, F.R. Ankersmit, Jean Wallach Scott, Agnes Heller, and Lynn Hunt.

Following Nietzsche's lead, for the most part, those within the more extreme camp of postmodernism deny the reality of an independently existing world as well as the possibility of true statements, or indeed, the possibility of any representation whatever of "the real," which is nothing more than a construct of many different worldviews. They tend to denigrate abstract and general statements and any attempt to build a systematic edifice that would "explain" human experience. As suggested above, they prefer immediate, personal, individual and/or group statements to grand philosophical systems. They deny that language refers to anything outside itself and insist that meaning is determined by arbitrary rules that are in constant flux. Life and everything in it is a "text," and what is interesting and important is what various people (especially the uninitiated) read into that text. In this regard, no one reading of the "text" is any "better" or any "worse" than another. Preference is possible, but not objective valuation, since this arbitrarily "privileges" one perspective over another.

These thinkers discard the subject/object dichotomy because it is, in their view, impossible to distinguish the world from its appearance to a "reader." History is reduced to myth and science to "someone's science" (Foucault). What is apparent to these thinkers, as it was to Nietzsche, is that underneath every attempt to establish truth can be found the desire for power.

There is a fundamental, systematic difficulty with the postmodern view, since most, if not all, of the claims in the above list are accepted as true by these people, who, at the same time, insist that there are no true claims. Jacques Derrida is one of the few in the group to face this paradox, and he simply agrees, as any good skeptic would, that his claims are also quite possibly false. Most others simply ignore the problem, but it is an even graver problem for the more militant camp within postmodernism, since those in this group want to advance political programs on grounds that disallow value judgments. Clearly, for example, if I want to advance the cause of feminism, I must assume that my point of view is somehow "correct" and that it is preferable to the antithetical position. That is, I must make truth claims and value judgments that I would insist are binding on other rational "readers." But I cannot do this if I have begun by saying that all claims are equally legitimate and none is to be privileged. This inconsistency is also disregarded, for the most part, and I shall have reason to reconsider it at some length later in the book as I look more carefully at the postmodern rejection of values. At the moment, it might help us to better understand the movement if we turn to one of its major sources of influence, Friedrich Nietzsche.

⁓

Nietzsche's idealism and obscurantism, his denial of the independent reality of "the world," and his love of paradox and surprise have played a large role in molding the thought of postmodern thinkers. Nietzsche is the one who first suggested that the world is a "text" to be read and interpreted by every "reader" in his or her own way (*Beyond Good and Evil* [*BGE*], 22, 230). It follows from this that there is no truth or knowledge because every reader must contend with his or her own values, interests, and goals, and these always interfere with every interpretation of "events." There is no reason to expect that these personal factors can be eliminated or that they are ultimately compatible. "Objectivity," viewed as neutrality or "contemplation without interest" is a false hope. "There is *only* perspective seeing, only perspective 'knowing'; and the *more* eyes, different eyes, we can use to observe one thing, the more complete will our 'concept' of this thing, our 'objectivity' be" (*Genealogy of Morals* [*GM*], III 12). In postmodernism, this leads directly to wholesale relativism and a tolerance for every possible interpretation with no grounds for making exceptions. In its desire to avoid dogmatism (with which one cannot quarrel, surely), postmodernism has followed Nietzsche into the trap of relativism, in which everyone's opinion has equal weight.[1] In Nietzsche's view, as Alexander Nehamas puts it, "Nietzsche's model for the world, for objects, and for people, turns out to be a literary text and its components; his model for our relation to the world turns out to be interpretation" (Nehamas 1985, 90). In a word, the world is anything we take it to be. It has no "essence." As Nietzsche himself put it, " 'Essence,' the 'essential nature,' is something perspectival and always presupposes a multiplicity. At the bottom of it there always lies 'what is it for me?' " (*Will to Power* [*WTP*], 556). "Reality," then, is a construct. That is to say, the only world we can talk about is the world we know, and our knowledge is ineluctably perspectival. Once again, we confront the question of whether there can be "correct" perspectives. Oddly, for Nietzsche, there are— as there are for his postmodern followers, if we attend carefully. Nietzsche himself says, for example, that "we must reject the Christian interpretation and condemn its 'meaning' as counterfeit" (*Gay Science* [*GS*], 357). Apparently, some perspectives are ruled out of court. This will not do. Nietzsche has run aground on the same systematic difficulty many of his followers have, as we saw above.

If reality is a construct of subjective perspectives and nothing more, then there are no grounds whatever for preferring one perspective over another. As we saw, Derrida is willing to accept this conclusion, but others in his camp simply ignore the problem and (like Nietzsche) continue to make prescriptive judgments and express their preferences. Clearly, in the view of most of these thinkers (including Derrida, in spite of his protestations to the contrary), some perspectives are "counterfeit"—presumably, those that conflict with their own. To avoid this intellectual impasse, we must have reference to an independent, objective world that stands over against the subject—though we must admit that reference to that world is tentative and always open to correction. This might become clearer if we examine the subjective/objective dichotomy in greater detail. Before turning to this examination, however, I would engage in a brief aside.

What Nietzsche really wants to insist upon—and correctly, in my view—is that no one is in a position to "privilege" his or her own perspective and claim that it is the *correct* way to view the world. This is especially true of the scientific worldview, as Nietzsche was careful to insist: "That the only justifiable interpretation of the world should be one in which *you* are justified because one can continue to work and do research scientifically in *your* sense (you really mean mechanistically?)—an interpretation that permits counting, calculating, weighing, seeing, and touching, and nothing more—that is a crudity and naivete, assuming that it is not mental illness, an idiocy." (*GS,* 373).

One can agree that it is essential to avoid dogmatism and narrow-mindedness without accepting Nietzsche's version of perspectivism. That is to say, we can accept the contention that the world can be viewed only perspectivally without accepting the conclusion that it is a *construct* made up of those perspectives. This does not commit us to the claim that any one perspective ought to be "privileged," but it allows us to avoid the absurdity of admitting that every perspective is equally legitimate. Clearly, some ways of seeing the world are superior to others—even though the views in question are in conflict with our own. Perspectives are not arbitrary, and although we cannot say with any finality which is "the correct" view of the world, we can agree with Charles Peirce that "the opinion which is fated to be ultimately agreed to by all who investigate is what we mean by truth, and the object represented in this opinion is real" (Peirce 1955, 38).

Venturing into the world of postmodernism is a bit like passing through the looking glass with Alice (except that what we find there is not terribly funny, unfortunately). As we have seen even in this brief overview, it is a topsy-turvy world where virtually every piece of the rationalistic framework of modernism has been shattered in favor of a new way of seeing the world (if, indeed, it is all that new). There is little doubt that much of the rejection of the modern logocentric paradigm is done for its own sake—that is, simply because it is modern or accords with what we have come to call "common sense."[2] Postmodern thinkers are clearly susceptible to exaggeration, reductionism, half-truth, and a kind of mysticism that clouds their vision and (almost always) their prose.

To be sure, many postmodern concerns are genuine and worthy of serious thought. The modern age began in great promise and optimism but has led to atomic bombs, nuclear waste, power in the hands of small-minded people, and widespread destruction of the environment. The certainty and outrageous optimism of Descartes (as expressed in the comment from *The Discourse on Method* quoted earlier in this chapter) have turned sour. But in their unqualified rejection of anything that smacks of human reason, postmodern thinkers would turn the world into a mindless mélange of subjective whimsy. This is unacceptable. We can avoid the Scylla of dogmatism that worries Nietzsche and most of the postmodern thinkers without sinking in the Charybdis of whimsy and relativistic nonsense.

There are several concerns arising from this overview that require immediate attention, since they directly impact on the thesis that this book will advance. I shall later suggest that values are real and a part of the "real world" independent of the one who makes value judgments. This is the view of "axiological realism," and it is clearly at odds with several claims of the postmodernists. I shall need to consider, then, their supposed rejection of "the real" as well as their reduction of the subjective/objective dichotomy that would make it impossible to speak about an "independent" world.

~

It is easier for philosophers in their closets to doubt the independent existence of objects than it is for, say, a person alone at night in a dark parking lot or a pilot whose main engine has just cut out over the Grand Canyon. But even though there are few idealists among these "common folk," the view does rest upon a genuine philosophical difficulty: how does one *know* that the object before oneself is "real" and not a figment of one's own imagination? The dichotomy between the object and the subject who (presumably) apprehends it was first put forward in a systematic way by Descartes, who gave us some hints about how we can legitimately distinguish between the mind— that which thinks, perceives, doubts, feels, and apprehends —and the body (object: literally "before the mind") that is thought, perceived, doubted, felt, or apprehended. Our language reflects the fundamental difference between an active subject and a passive object. As Hume noted, the object is independent of the subject because it is not manipulable at will; we cannot make it disappear simply because we want it to. The point is well stated by a recent author discussing what he calls "postcivilized modernity." He reminds us that "even if I admit that I have access only to my version of the world, I assert even more confidently that it is not my world, that things are not the way I would like them to be" (Weinstein 1995, 32).

Phenomenologically, one need only reflect on present consciousness to realize its basic polarity, the dual nature of the subject who is conscious and the object of which the subject is conscious. I am always conscious of *something:* consciousness is intentional. In saying this, I would also note that it is quite possible to make an object of the subject itself, as when I say, "I feel a trifle nauseated at the moment," or "I am tall and of average weight." The predicates can be multiplied ad infinitum, but they are nothing less than attempts to objectify the subject—while the subject itself remains (always) that which actively reflects upon itself. In the end, however, the subject and the object are inherently different, and even in borderline cases in which, for example, a person feels pain in a limb that has been amputated, the subject is that which remains conscious of something not of itself. There is something stubborn and persistent about the real world that is not a product of our own imagination. In any event, we need not concern ourselves with borderline cases, since, as Monroe Beardsley has noted, the experience of "phenomenal objectivity" carries with it a degree of self-evidence that is usually beyond question (Beardsley 1958, 35).

Idealism, like skepticism, rests upon the fact that we cannot *prove* that objects are real (i.e., exist independently of the subject). We cannot know it beyond the shadow of a doubt. But outside of logic and arithmetic, "knowing" is seldom "proving," and skepticism fades when confronted by cumulative experience over time. This cumulative experience allows us to attach a very high probability to our claims that the book in your hands is real and not a fiction. In the "real world," probabilities are the best we can hope for, and the claim that objects in that world are real is most probable.

One can also speak of objectivity in another sense, of course. One can speak of *claims* that are objective to the extent that they can be verified or disproved by independent persons. A subjective claim, on the other hand, lacks the evidence necessary to verify it and amounts to little more than personal opinion. I shall explore this sense of objectivity in greater detail in a later chapter. For the moment, suffice it to say that, in both cases, objectivity connotes independence from the subject, either through its presence to the subject and consequent independence of his or her will, or through the evidence that supports a claim and renders it "reasonable" or "true." In a word, we can agree with what is most important in the postmodern view—to wit, that *knowledge* is perspectival—without accepting the view that *reality* is a construct made up of individual perspectives.

Postmodernists would, of course, deny the legitimacy of my entire analysis because of its reliance on reasonability and notions such as "probability" and "truth." Their contention, as we have seen, is that truth is a matter (at best) of convention and for the most part arbitrary. But it is difficult to see how this is so when truth and objectivity obtrude themselves into our consciousness and lay claim to our assent whether or not we want to give it. Unlike the world of ideas, there is, as Peirce noted long ago, "an element of brute compulsion" in our confrontation with the real world (Peirce 1934, 5:97).

The issue is not quite this simple, of course. Not only do postmodern thinkers insist that reality and truth are constructs; they make the further claim that groups employ their version of "truth" to gain and maintain power over others. This is another footnote to Nietzsche's claim that truth is power. Alphonso Lingis has put the point rather dramatically:

> Truth requires institutions that select researchers, teach them paradigms of successful research, and train them to repeat and apply that research to batches of other material se-

lected by institutional criteria; it requires institutions that certify and evaluate their researchers and technicians. It requires institutions that select what research is to be published and how it is to be judged. All these institutions recruit and train their members and are funded and controlled by institutions that regulate the command posts by which the established community monopolizes and elaborates its power. (Lingis 1994, 136)

This statement is typical of the blend of insight with exaggeration and half-truth that one finds in the works of so many postmodern thinkers. At the center of this statement lies an important kernel of truth and round about it the rhetorical flotsam and jetsam of hyperbole.

Even a casual look at the history of science will reveal that institutions played almost no role whatever in the origins of the scientific method and current claims about the nature of truth. Thinkers such as Copernicus, Tycho Brahe, Kepler, Galileo, and Descartes—not to mention Francis Bacon—had sponsors who kept them alive. Several of these men made a living as court astrologers, but their patrons cared little about the astronomical speculations these men engaged in during their spare hours. On the whole, they were left alone, with occasional interference by the Roman church—the only "institution" on the scene and one that was *opposed* to the new notions of truth. What "institution" dictated the move from scholastic to empirical methodology? What "institution" coerced Isaac Newton into gathering together the pieces handed to him by these men and writing his *Principia?* The notion that "institutions" drove these events and determined the outcomes in order to enhance their hegemony is bogus. To be sure, knowledge is power, and it is tempting to misuse power. Furthermore, it is certainly the case that institutions play a much greater role today than they did in the early days of modern science. Nevertheless, although it may be true that they influence research, it is an exaggeration to insist that these institutions control the researchers' minds.

But Lingis's suggestion, which echoes a theme one finds running through much of postmodern thought, is that truth is determined by those in power in order to control those who are purposely deceived and kept at a distance. This suggestion is based on distortion.

Truth is determined in accordance with the scientific method—and rational schemes that are modeled after the scientific method. This method was devised, as noted, by a small group of determined men working, for the most part, independently of one another with little or no institutional influence whatever. These methods yield claims that can be verified by anyone with the time and inclination to repeat the experiments. Truth has reference to a world we share in common and with which claims must conform in a manner susceptible to independent verification.

The fact that the "world" can only be apprehended by means of our ideas of it poses perplexing philosophical problems but few practical problems—as the success of science attests. The fact that our ideas stand between us and an independent reality does not mean that we cannot lay claim to knowledge about that reality, even though the extent of those knowledge claims can always be questioned.

To be sure, there is a prescriptive element in the "approved" methods of determining truth. Historical claims that are considered true because they make us feel good but that fail to meet rigorous standards of evidence will be rejected. And indeed, they should. Psychologists will remain suspicious of claims about extrasensory perception and paranormal behavior until these phenomena can be subjected to controlled experiments. Physicists will remain skeptical about the claims of extraterrestrial visits until the evidence becomes weighty enough to jettison the counter-arguments. But these restrictions about what counts as "true" are the results of years of pragmatic success that have resulted in a coherent worldview that makes understanding and prediction possible. It is prudent not to set them aside simply because they yield results that sometimes make us feel uncomfortable or because we find them exclusive. It is even more prudent not to set them aside simply because the claim is made that they yield a truth that is designed by one group to control another. This is especially the case since we don't know what we are supposed to substitute for methods that have yielded such spectacular results since the seventeenth century—despite the misuses to which they have been put.

What is the alternative to the scientific method and the rational pursuit of an elusive truth? Whimsy? "Feel-good" history? "New Age" scientology? Can we really take seriously the claims of these marginal thinkers that truth is nothing more than what we make it out to be? Surely not. Truth is referential, and its claims are intersubjectively verifiable, despite the fact, acknowledged above, that both language and truth can be abused to manipulate the unwary.

What we have in Lingis's suggestion is what might be called an "institutional" theory of truth. Its plausibility is a function of its idealistic presuppositions. If they are rejected and we insist that true claims refer beyond themselves to a real world—difficult though that may be to "prove"—we can reasonably reject this theory of truth. If we insist, as we must, that truth is not arbitrary and the methods whereby it is determined are not whimsical, we can avoid the extremism implied in this version of truth as power. Of central importance is the critical stance of the researchers—some of whom, even today, are not members of any institutions —and all of whom must be willing to critique their own methodologies. If researchers maintain a critical stance, then the capacity of "truth" to "elaborate power" is severely constrained. In a word, if claims must always be tested by reference to a world that resists our arbitrary determinations, those claims and the people who make them do not have carte blanche to make of the world what they will.

Clearly, there is something to what Lingis says about the abuses of power and its relation to truth. There is reason to be suspicious of truth that has become institutionalized, especially when these institutions are self-serving. However, one senses in thinkers like Lingis, and his predecessor Michel Foucault, traces of the hysteria that lies at the root of Nietzsche's epistemology. Accordingly, one must be on one's guard not only against institutionalized truth but also against those who rail against institutions. It is one thing to be cautious, and even a bit cynical, and it is quite another to reject all truth as manufactured by arbitrary methods invented by unscrupulous people to control the ignorant. In the end, truth must be grounded in the world, no matter how difficult it is to find our way there.

It is necessary at this point to consider more carefully the postmodern rejection of reason, as this is a key to my major concern with postmodernism.

The rejection of reason is based on three major concerns and is said to be a part of a "larger erosive trend" in society generally. The first concern is that "modern reason assumes universalism, unifying integration, the view that the same rules apply everywhere" (Rosenau 1992, 128). Postmodernism rejects these views, as we have seen, but if the grounds for this rejection are that they are "unreasonable," we are caught in a vicious circle. Indeed, we can just as easily reject postmodernism's argument on the grounds that it *denies* universalism, integration, and the application of the same rules everywhere. It is not self-evident that these things are undesirable. Indeed, it is considerably more likely that they are desirable than it is that we should fall back upon whimsy and personal perspectives.

The second and third concerns, though, are more serious and to a degree more legitimate. The second concern is that "reason is the product of the Enlightenment, modern science, and Western society, and as such for the postmodernists, it is guilty by association of all the errors attributed to them, [namely], violence, suffering, and alienation in the twentieth century, be it the Holocaust, world wars, Vietnam, Stalin's Gulag, or computer record-keeping . . ." (Rosenau 1992, 129).

Although this is a serious concern, it is hardly grounds for the rejection of reason, for which postmodernism calls in a loud, frenetic voice. There is precious little evidence that the problems of the twentieth century are the result of too much reason! On the contrary. To be sure, it was Descartes's dream to reduce every decision to a calculation, and in ethics, this dream bore fruit in Jeremy Bentham's abortive "calculus" of utilities. But at least since the birth of the social sciences at the end of the last century, and with considerable help from logical positivism, ethics (and values in general) has been relegated to the dung heap of "poetical and metaphysical nonsense," and in the minds of the general populace, reason has no place in ethics, which is the proper domain of *feeling*. The postmodern concern to place feelings at the center of ethics, and judgment generally—which is the third of their three objections to modern reason—simply plays into the hands of the hardened popular prejudice that has little respect for the abilities of human beings to resolve moral differences reasonably.

Can it honestly be said of any major decision made in this century that it was the result of "too much reason" and that feelings and emotions played no part? Surely not. Can this be said in the case of any of the concerns reflected in the list above: are violence, suffering, and alienation, or the Holocaust, Vietnam, Stalin's Gulag, or Auschwitz the result of a too reasonable approach to human problems? No one could possibly make this claim who has dared to peek into the dark and turbid recesses of the human psyche. In every case, it is more likely that these concerns result from such things as sadism, envy, avarice, love of power, the "death wish," or short-term self-interest, none of which is "reasonable."

One must carefully distinguish between the methods of

the sciences, which are thoroughly grounded in reason and logic, and the uses men and women make of science. The warnings of romantics such as Goethe (who was himself no mean scientist) and Mary Shelley were directed not against science *per se* but rather against the misuse of science and the human tendency to become embedded in the operations of the present moment. To the extent that postmodernism echoes these concerns, I would share them without hesitation. But the claim that our present culture suffers because of an exclusive concern with "reasonable" solutions to human problems, with a fixation on the logos, borders on the absurd.

What is required here is not a mindless rejection of human reason on behalf of "intuition," "conscience," or "feelings" in the blind hope that somehow complex problems will be solved if we simply do whatever makes us feel good. Feelings and intuitions are notoriously unreliable and cannot be made the center of a workable ethic. We now have witnessed several generations of college students who are convinced that "there's no disputing taste" in the arts and that ethics is all about feelings. As a result, it is almost impossible to get them to take these issues seriously. The notion that we can trust our feelings to find solutions to complex problems is little more than a false hope.

We are confronted today with problems on a scale heretofore unknown, and what is called for is patience, compassion (to be sure), and above all else, clear heads. In a word, what is called for is a balance between reason and feelings—not the rejection of one or the other. One need only recall Nietzsche's own concern for the balance between Dionysus and Apollo in his *Birth of Tragedy*. Nietzsche knew better than his followers, apparently, that one cannot sacrifice Apollo to Dionysus in the futile hope that we can rely on our blind instincts to get us out of the hole we have dug for ourselves.

~

To say, as I have, that the basic tenets of postmodernism are unacceptable is not to imply that these thinkers have nothing worthwhile to say. This is simply not the case. Despite the fact that much of what they have written is (by design) expressed in an opaque style (since this allows for so many more diverse interpretations) and that reading some of the major works can be like swimming in glue, there is much that is interesting and a number of important points to bear in mind. The postmodern view of language is a case in point, though here, too, I shall have to dissent from unqualified acceptance of the postmodern view. But surely, these thinkers are correct in noting the many ways that language can enable one person to have and maintain power over another.

Language encloses, it snares and entraps. When, for example, I say, "Harry is a short, bald man," I say what Harry is and what he is not. I separate that part of the world that "Harry is" from that which "he is not." When simple statements begin to compound and theories or ways of viewing the world evolve, they have the power to seduce us into a way of seeing that becomes a way of being in the world. This may be called the "seductive" power of language, and it is clearly a form that power of one person over another can take, especially if these forms become institutionalized.

This concern is at the center of the current controversy about "political correctness," which is a matter worthy of serious consideration.

Though a concern for this type of power can also become exaggerated, authors such as Gilles Deleuze and Felix Guattari have done a masterful job of demonstrating how in the case of Sigmund Freud all of psychoanalysis has become surrounded and boxed in by the schema and categories of the Oedipus myth. And to the extent to which analysts themselves accept this myth, they use it to maintain control over their patients.

The Freudian schemata are reductionistic and tend to simplify human motivations, to reduce them to pat formulations and familiar ways of thinking. Indeed, these authors would contend, language in general does this. Thus, we must beware the many traps and pitfalls of language that can dupe us into thinking we understand because we can *identify,* even though we cannot discuss coherently and systematically. To the extent that postmodern thinkers are reminding us of these things, what they say is of central importance.

On a mundane level, through the manipulation of language, advertising daily gets people to do what they do not necessarily want to do. We have all become convinced that we have "needs" that go beyond our biological needs and conflict at times with the needs of the spirit (which are largely ignored in our "commodified" culture). In the name of satisfying these "needs" we find ourselves racing for the sake of increased purchasing power to satisfy ever-growing, seemingly insatiable "needs" for consumer goods. We become enslaved by the symbols of conspicuous consumption.

It will not do to object that the example of American consumerism fails to show how language translates into power, because most (if not all) of the people who go into debt to purchase more and more "things" *want* to do so and therefore do so by "their own free will." This argument simply shows a rather naive attitude toward power and about human freedom. Michel Foucault is perhaps at his best in destroying this naiveté and showing the subtleties of power. As Foucault puts it, "What makes power hold good, what makes it accepted, is simply the fact that it doesn't only weigh on us as a force that says no, but that it traverses and produces things, it induces pleasure, forms knowledge, produces discourse. It needs to be considered as a productive network which runs through the whole social body, much more than as a negative instance whose function is repression" (Foucault 1984, 61).

Although it is certainly not the case that all advertising, for example, is "persuasive"—which is to say that it operates by means of "hidden persuaders"—it is nonetheless the case that much of it is, especially when directed at children. It is an important and interesting topic for continued investigation as to how it is that those who control the sources of information are able to control the thoughts of presumably "free" men and women. Any further discussion of this topic, however, would take us too far afield and is unnecessary, since it was addressed in 1958 by Aldous Huxley in *Brave New World*.

As necessary as studies of the power of language are, however, and as brilliant as some of them that have already been produced in France and America are, it is easy to succumb to the siren song of the voices that generate the critical studies themselves. They can readily lead to their own kind of entrapment. It is one thing to say that language is seductive and threatens at every turn to ensnare the mind; it is another to say that we cannot avoid these snares and pitfalls. The way out is through education, properly understood, and we must also stress the referential nature of language. Meanings do not arise from rules, simply; they also refer to the world that ultimately grounds language and meaning. I shall develop this theme in greater detail in later chapters.

In the end, I must admit that I am in sympathy with some of what the postmodernists are trying to do. Ours is indeed a sick culture in need of a cure. We seem to have succumbed to the temptations of scientism, whereby all questions will be answered in terms that can be measured in graduated cylinders. This is an affectation of our culture, and to the extent that postmodernism attempts to relocate our cultural center, one cannot dissent.

As a movement, postmodernism has its roots deep within the European world that gave rise to modern science: in the romanticism of Herder and Goethe, if not even deeper in Shakespeare. And this at a time when science was aborning and so many were becoming swept up by the fascination with science and its promise to solve all problems and answer every question.

Nietzsche, to whom so many postmodern thinkers trace their sources, built on a tradition that was already quite old at his birth and espoused by some of the greatest minds in western Europe. The movement to dethrone the "despised logos" is not new, and it is based on serious and legitimate concerns. But like so much of postmodernism, it must be accompanied by a healthy respect for the accomplishments of reason and science and an unrelenting desire to achieve balance.

One cannot gainsay much of the spirit of postmodernism to the extent that it presents itself within a tradition that exhibits such impressive credentials. What one can fault, however, are the cadres of hangers-on who mouth the platitudes and memorize the jargon but who evince little or no real sympathy for, or knowledge of, the tradition that waters the roots of the postmodern movement itself.

The (highly logical and reasonable) work by such thinkers as Derrida in deconstructing texts shows us how dangerous it is to presume to know and how many are the possibilities of meanings in any text. As we have seen, *Anti-Oedipus* shows us how we can become ensnared in our myths and metaphors and how language can be used as a tool for enslavement.

Having said this much, however, I must note again that there exist alongside the insights and telling observations elements of hysteria and exaggeration in the views of these people, who see in language nothing else than relationships of power and control—as if language were simply a tool to be manipulated at will by the user, writer, or speaker. This sort of reduction ignores the element of reference to our common world that severely restricts our abilities to manipulate language at will. Language is a tool, and it can become a weapon: it governs to a large extent the way we view our common world. But its power is limited, as is the power of those who would abuse it, by the fact that meaning is determined—in part, at least—by reference to that world.

Notes

1. Alexander Nehamas has attempted to rescue Nietzsche's perspectivism from relativism, but without success. He insists that "Perspectivism does not result in the relativism that holds that any view is as good as any other, it holds that one's own views are the best for oneself without implying that they need to be any good for anyone else" (Nehamas 1985, 92). The author of this comment makes a distinction without a difference here. Relativism is, in fact, the view that "one's own view is best for oneself," as contrasted with objectivism, which would insist that if it is true for me, it is also true for you. The only way to avoid relativism is to insist that perspectives are different ways of viewing the *same* thing, that the "thing" is not created by readers or spectators but that they each have different ways of seeing the same object. Thus, one can accept Nietzsche's perspectivism without falling into the trap of relativism, but only by rejecting his ontology. This is what I attempt to do in this book.

2. There is an amusing anecdote in a footnote in Pauline Marie Rosenau's book that recounts the attempts by an "avant-garde postmodern architect" who "took great pride in 'knowing nothing about materials,'" and who subsequently designed an officers' club only to have "the roof cave in during the dedication ceremonies" (Rosenau 1992, 120 n. 30). Is this event, perhaps, symbolic?

Chapter 3

The Rejection of Values

Ours is an age that is instinct with hatred of values.
—Eliseo Vivas

In the last chapter, I discussed briefly the "postmodern challenge" to the independent existence of values and truth about our common world. The challenge rests on a faulty reduction of reality to appearance, a misguided rejection of "the despised logos," and the conviction that modernism is spiritually bankrupt. As I have suggested, there are some important truths at the heart of this position, but we must be cautious in turning our backs on a tradition that may offer us the only way out of our present quagmire. In much of the discussion about our present crisis, conclusions are hastily drawn, and hyperbole and half-truths are sometimes mistaken for insight and wisdom.

In this chapter, I want to examine a small part of the American branch of postmodernism that has tended to focus attention on the question of values. In particular, I want to examine carefully one very thoughtful rejection of value by an American postmodern critic who is guilty of reducing value to evaluation, since this is my particular concern in this book. Later in the chapter, I shall expand my discussion to an examination of the wholesale rejection of values in our culture, particularly as it relates to ethics. My hope is to pave the way for a thorough discussion of the nature of value and a defense of value in ethics and aesthetics.

I

In their stubborn insistence that the meaning of literary works is arbitrarily grounded in the shifting contingencies of reader response, rather than in the works themselves, the demystifiers of postmodern criticism bear a striking resemblance to the owners of the wine casks in the Cervantes parable recounted at the start of this book. The difference in this case, however, is that when the key is produced, these critics insist with casual indifference that the existence of the key on its thong and the ability of the wine tasters to detect the metal and the leather are sheer coincidence. More to the point, a developed taste among readers of books that finds some better than others is also coincidental; and when it becomes institutionalized, it forms what might be called a "conspiracy" among those in a position to make such judgments and impose them on the rest of us.

Of greater interest and concern, however, are the claims these critics make about the texts that are put forward as somehow deserving of serious attention, texts that are exceptional or even, perhaps, "great." We are told that such evaluations are suspect: they reflect nothing more than the personal attitudes and preferences of the readers and tell us nothing about the texts themselves. Some critics go even further and deny that there exist such things as "texts" at all.

In opposing these views, I shall argue that not only do literary texts exist, but some are better than others and can legitimately be considered great. Further, some readers are in a better position than others to recognize greatness in literature: in this respect, they resemble Sancho's relatives. When all is said and done, it is arrant nonsense to continue to insist that the wine contains no key once the cask is dry and the evidence stares us in the face.

~

I shall begin by focusing attention on some of the claims made by Barbara Herrnstein Smith in her important book *Contingencies of Value,* because I consider it to be the work of one of the best minds among the current crop of postmodern critics in America. I shall then turn to several other critics of stature, but if I am to rescue great literature from the heirs of Roland Barthes, Smith's claims must be addressed.

The title of Smith's book reveals her preoccupation with evaluation. The "contingency" of value is a function of the contingency of culturally grounded responses to works we call "good" or "bad," "great" or "not so great." She shares with many other postmodern critics the conviction that judgments of value in general, and determinations of what works will compose "the canon" in particular, are ultimately arbitrary. They are a product of a conspiracy among those engaged in "establishment axiology," chiefly white males in positions of authority (Smith 1988, 40). Her attention is focused on what she calls the particular "economies" of the establishment axiologists: specifically, "the personal economy constituted by the subject's needs, interests, and resources—biological, psychological, material, experiential, and so forth" (Smith 1988, 30).

The idea that there are qualities inherent in the objects themselves she rejects out of hand. As she notes in this regard,

> [I]t is precisely under these conditions that the value of particular objects will appear to be inherent, that distinctions or gradations of value among them will appear to reduce to differences in the "properties" or "qualities" of the objects themselves, and that explicit judgments of their value will appear to be—and for many, but not all, purposes *will* be—"objective." In short, here as elsewhere, *a co-incidence of contingencies among individual subjects who interact as members of some community will operate for them as noncontingency and be interpreted by them accordingly.* (Smith 1988, 39; italics in original)

This is where the conspiracy enters the picture: it is the result of the "co-incidence of contingencies" among those who happen to be in a position to impose their own sense of what is a great work of art on those who do not exhibit "good taste." Whatever agreement there happens to be among "establishment axiologists" must simply be a coincidence, because there is nothing about which to agree: there are no grounds for the judgments we make about works of art, either in the objects themselves or in the subjective conditions of evaluation. There are simply personal preferences and the coordination of preferences among those in positions of prestige who maintain power by denying legitimacy to the judgments of those who disagree with them. Notice how this view accords with Alphonso Lingis's "institutional" theory of truth as discussed in the last chapter.

What I am talking about now is what Smith refers to as "privileging absolutely" the preferences of so-called experts among establishment axiologists. That is, we have uncovered the phenomenon of "standardizing," which is, in Smith's view, "making a standard out of—not simply the preferences of the members of the group but, more significantly and more powerfully because more invisibly, *the particular contingencies that govern their preferences;* and, second but simultaneously, *discounting and pathologizing* not merely other people's tastes but, again more significantly and effectively, *all other contingencies*" (Smith 1988, 41; italics in original).

In such a world, "the texts that survive will tend to be those that appear to reflect and reinforce establishment ideologies" (Smith 1988, 51). We have, at last, uncovered the deadly worm of elitism that lurks near the heart of establishment axiology. And of all evils, Smith is most intent on exorcising this one.

Because appreciation of great works of art (among which I would include great works of literature) requires what John Dewey called a "transaction" between subject and object, it is hard to deny much of what Smith says about the "contingencies" of value. To be sure, we do not confront great works of art and literature as empty vessels to be filled. We bring our preferences and biases, our stupidity and insensitivity, our color blindness and our tone deafness, our axes to grind and our hidden agendas—all of which influence our judgments about what does and does not constitute "great" art. This is the baggage we bring with us into the library, art gallery, and theater: much of it is useless; it is often packed for us at night while we sleep; and at times, it obscures our judgment. Smith's mistake, however, is to dwell on the subjective and ignore the objective pole of the transaction. This becomes particularly clear in one of the rare instances in Smith's book when she actually considers a great work of literature, or at least a great poet. In speaking of Homer she notes that "what may be spoken of as the 'properties' of a work—its 'structure,' 'features,' 'qualities,' and of course its 'meanings'—are not fixed, given, or inherent in the work 'itself' but are at every point the variable products of particular *subjects'* interactions with it. Thus it is never the *same* Homer" (Smith 1988, 48; italics in original).

To be sure, as people and their valuations change over time, different readers will "see" a work differently. But this does not mean that Homer's vision changed with that of his readers. Texts do not vary with their readers; readers vary in their responses to texts. This is my theme.

⁓

At the outset, however, it must be noted that the heart of much postmodern criticism lies in the deconstructionist denial of the "text" as something that exists independently of the reader. The rejection stems from Roland Barthes's notion of the "writerly text" that has no central meaning but is rewritten every time it is read (Barthes 1975, 77). In order to confront directly the postmodern rejection of the ideal of greatness in literature, I will have to deal with this issue.

The text, we are told, is nothing more than a construct generated anew with each reading, a construct that merely reflects what Smith called the various "economies" of the readers. As SueEllen Campbell has noted, somewhat defiantly, "without a reader, the words on the page mean nothing—we give them life with our feelings, our experience, our knowledge, our subjectivity" (Campbell 1989, 204). Similarly, in denying that there is any "ahistorical, transcendent text" that calls forth the variety of interpretations we associate with, say, *Hamlet,* Jane Tompkins argues:

> In each case, the reading can be accounted for by a series of quite specific, documentable circumstances having to do with publishing practices, pedagogical and critical traditions, economic structures, social networks, and national needs which constitute the text within the framework of a particular disciplinary hermeneutic.... [T]he text ... is not durable at all. What endures is the literary and cultural tradition that believes in the idea of the classic, and that perpetuates that belief from day to day and from year to year.... (Tompkins 1994, 127)

Thus, there is no *Hamlet,* there are many *Hamlet*s, and the fact that "the work" survives merely testifies to the power of "establishment axiologists" to protect "texts" that they happen to prefer, presumably because those "texts" reinforce their view of culture and protect their hegemony. Although there is an element of truth in this position, it is, once again, a half-truth.

The "ahistorical, transcendent text" does exist. I can get it from my library and order it from my bookstore. So can you. It will be argued that this is not the text, it is the book: they are not the same. This is (perhaps) a legitimate distinction, but it does not solve our problem. Even if we "bracket" the question of the reality of the words that are the object of our consciousness while we are reading, nonetheless there is that which *subtends* the multiplicity of judgments we all make about that object—like Descartes's lump of wax that remains the same after he moves it closer to the fire and all the qualities of the wax change. That is, the text and its objectivity are made evident by the coherence of the judgments about it and the diversity of subjects who are able to discuss the *same* thing. When the deconstructionist, the feminist, the psychoanalytic, and the Marxist critics talk about *Hamlet,* we know what they are talking *about.* Put simply, they are talking about the same text in different ways.

Many deconstructionists, not including Jacques Derrida, would deny that this is "the text" at all, since the text is nothing more than what people make of it, and it is different things to different people. But this claim is either a tautology or materially false, because, in point of fact, the words we read and hear are the basis for every possible interpretation. They are what we come back to time and again as we try to determine what *it* means. William Gass has explained how readers mold characters, for example, and how, later on, "meanings, uncovered, must be put back as they were found. It is a delicate operation" (Gass 1977, 46). Indeed, the meanings in the text ground the possibilities of interpretation.

Let me suggest an example from music. A great composer "hears" music in her mind. She writes out the music in mathematical symbols—that is, the accepted system of musical notation. Let's say it's a waltz, and we all know waltzes are written in ¾ time. The composer dies. A century later, someone discovers the piece in an attic and sits down to play it on the piano. The music was not in the printed symbols on the paper. But that abstract set of symbols held together the music's possibilities.

So, too, with the printed words of a novel. The text provides the possibilities of meanings being communicated from writer to reader. The text is symbolic meaning in transition, as it were. The musical composition dictates the conditions for the possibilities of the music and sets limits on those possibilities. The waltz will still be a waltz in ¾ time a century later, not a sonata or a fugue. And the mood, tone, and melodic line are set by the abstract symbols the composer wrote down, not by what happens to be in the head of a listener a century later, though the listener must have some skill in listening in order to encounter the music properly. The same process, for the most part, operates between writer and reader of a fictional text.

The novelist uses words selected with great care and attention. We cannot ignore either what the novelist has said or the manner of saying it. Separating the text from the author's words is a bit like peeling an orange: what you have in the end are bits and pieces; you can stick them back together to look like they once did, but they are still bits and pieces—and it's all hollow inside. The text is the object that exists in print; and it is *also* in the reader's mind while it is being read.

As hinted above, theorists within the postmodern camp are not in agreement on this issue. Barthes, we recall, insists that the "writerly" text is open to innumerable interpretations. Jacques Derrida, on the other hand, simply insists that the text is heterogeneous, a nexus of possible readings. Recalling Nietzsche's rejection of "the Christian interpretation," Derrida, for instance, rejects the "mimetic perversion" of the Nazi readings of Nietzsche's works that allows the reader to "bend them to its own purpose" (Norris 1987, 201). Interpretation, according to Derrida, is "not a free-for-all of relativism." Derrida is surely correct, and his rejection of other interpretations as "wrong," like Nietzsche's, implies a core of meaning that becomes the standard for possible future interpretations.

The reduction of the text to any possible version of what we read makes it impossible to explain how a poem like the *Iliad* can last for more than two thousand years and continue to be experienced in ways that are not totally unlike the ways the Athenians themselves almost certainly experienced the same poem long ago. Barbara Herrnstein Smith asserts, somewhat flippantly, that "it is never the *same* Homer." In an obvious sense, it is not. But in important respects, it most assuredly is—even for those who cannot read Greek. If we could resurrect an ancient Athenian, the problems we might have in communicating with him about the *Iliad* would not differ in any important respect from the difficulty many of us would have today in discussing the Koran with a Muslim.

The fact that we do *communicate* about the text goes to the heart of the matter. The text is what we talk about. There is something *there* that brings readers back repeatedly despite changing times and circumstances. The postmodern rejection of the text smacks of bifurcation: either the text is precisely the same once and for all, or there is no text. This is simplistic.

In the midst of the multiplicity of interpretations, we find works that we continue to take seriously even after the seemingly relentless assault by every heavy weapon in the postmodern arsenal. This is a phenomenon that is frustrating to some reductionistic thinkers but one that also calls for explanation. As Marjorie Garber has asked regarding *Hamlet,*

> Why do we still maintain the centrality of Shakespeare? Why in a time of canon expansion and critique of canonical literature does Shakespeare not only remain unchallenged, but in fact emerge newly canonized . . . ? Why with the current renaissance in Renaissance studies, is Shakespeare still the touchstone for new historicists, feminists, deconstructors? Why, in other words, do those who criticize canonical authority so often turn to Shakespeare to ratify the authority of their critique? (Wofford 1994, 298)

In response, I would respectfully suggest that despite all the talk, in the end, the text will simply not disappear. *Hamlet* remains because it is a great play and it continues to speak to us despite the fact that every age "reinvents" Shakespeare. The permanence of this particular play is not merely a matter of coincidence, nor is it a result of a conspiracy among critics. We can do better than that. Its greatness is in its language and its ability to touch those of us who know what it means to be torn apart by ethical conflict.

The followers of Nietzsche, Derrida, and Barthes mine for richness that lies deep within human consciousness, pressed there by decades of tradition, repetition, and ritual obeisance. They would remove the layers of meanings that have been built up over the years. For Derrida, at any rate, the challenge is to find a new way to read these texts in order to ferret out meanings that are hidden under old ways of reading. This is a worthy project, indeed. In the process, however, it is easy to ignore the sources that triggered the original awareness: the texts, the performances, and the events. There is no question but that these miners after hidden awareness are justified in their search. There is much to be gained, but there is much to lose as well. In their determination to destroy the hated "logos," they perform a series of reductions that raise serious questions about their entire project. What we have heard and seen and experienced over the centuries was initiated by something *out there* in the world, and we turn our backs on the sources of human experience at the cost of becoming tangled in human constructions and losing contact with the real world. As Jacques Derrida himself noted in this regard, "To distance oneself from the habitual structure of reference, to challenge or complicate our common assumptions about it, does not amount to saying that there is *nothing* beyond language" (Kearney 1984, 124).

The problem to which I am alluding is a manifestation of what I called in the first chapter "inverted consciousness." We do not create our world; we discover it. Of course, that discovery may well be creative: it is certainly the case that we respond to that world and interpret its various meanings. But it is no less certain that there is a world both rich and valuable of which we are a part and which we did not make.

Among the victims of this reductionistic enterprise are the features of objects and aspects of events that fill our common world—namely, the values that, as I shall argue, "require" affirmation and approval. If we follow postmodern criticism, we are left bereft of great literature, noble actions, beautiful works of art, breathtaking spectacles, and all sense of a common culture that centers the Western world.

It is no less a mistake, to be sure, to reduce the whole world of human experience to Western (European) culture. But while we acknowledge the legitimacy of other ways of looking at our world, I would insist that we confront the *same* world—no matter how diverse our responses may be. The egalitarian sentiment that insists upon diversity as the only value must not obscure the plethora of other values that make some of the diversity worthwhile—and much of it worthless. Many of these values arise from within the Western tradition, and many do not, but they are all values whose source is outside the self that apprehends them.

The postmodern reduction of value to evaluation is merely a part of a larger reductionistic tendency that has been prevalent since the birth of the social sciences and the growth of scientism. This view has a tenacious hold on a popular imagination that insists values are the result of enculturation: as such, they are beyond dispute.

II

The view that values are embedded within the cultures where they are found is called cultural relativism. In this view, values have no application outside that culture, and it is impossible to understand, much less critique, those values from another cultural perspective.

At first glance, this view makes perfectly good sense. We know enough about the great variety of cultures present and past to appreciate the fact that people disagree widely about what is valuable and what is worthless, what they ought to do and what they ought not to do, what is good and what is evil. One culture practices genocide against the aged because it regards the elderly as a threat to the survival of the young, whereas another culture reveres the aged because they have lived a long time and are considered wise in the ways of the world. In our frantic quest for tolerance at any price—even if it costs us the truth—we acknowledge differences and stop there. We insist that the values reflected in the different attitudes toward the elderly, in this case, are a product of "enculturation" and that "everyone is entitled to his or her own opinion"—a statement that is intended to mean that what one culture takes to be right or wrong is, in fact, right or wrong as far as it is given to human beings to determine these things. No attempt to judge a particular culture to be in error in its apprehension of right and wrong can be made from another cultural perspective.

For the moment, I shall ignore the confusion in this view between what people *think* is the case and what is the case *in fact* in order to turn my attention to the glaring half-truth that occurs in the final claim in the above paragraph: if one judges the attitudes of people in a given culture toward the elderly to be "mistaken," one must do so from another cultural perspective—namely, one's own. This much is true. However, it does not follow from this that all such judgments are fraudulent.

The question can be raised whether or not one's judgment about the attitudes of the people in another culture is *simply* a matter of enculturation, whether it *simply* reflects one's own cultural biases *and nothing more*. It is this claim that is susceptible to criticism, because it is much too simple.

One might, for example, examine the basis of the judgment of people in a given culture toward the elderly and determine that it is based on fear or misunderstanding about the aging process and the question of the usefulness of the aged in helping to raise young children. Similarly, one might judge the attitudes of the Hitler Youth toward the Jews to be based on a myth about racial inferiority that cannot be defended on rational grounds. One can do this also in the case of the Iroquois who considered their enemies to be "inferior" and tried to confirm this by testing their endurance to torture; also in the case of the white bigot who never questions his superiority to black people. Examples multiply. We know, for instance, that traditional Chinese culture bound the feet of its women because the men liked small feet. As a result, the women became hobbled and at times could not walk. The traditional Masai culture in Africa practiced female castration in order to foster female subjugation. If we regard these practices as perverse, is our judgment simply a reflection of our own cultural bias? Or are these practices indefensible on any grounds other than the consideration that they are practiced by those cultures? Such grounds seem hardly adequate to build a case.

The judgment of the Iroquois, the Hitler Youth, the Masai, the Chinese, and the bigot all rest on a confusion about the worth of persons. Additionally, there are often distortions of fact that purportedly support value judgments, and such claims can be summarily dismissed. Values, as we shall see in the next chapter, are related systemically to other features of the world that are factual—that is, open to independent investigation and corroboration by anyone at any time. They are not merely a reflection of personal or cultural perspective. It is therefore not enough to dismiss an objection to a value claim with a repetition of the mantra "You can't possibly know because you don't live there." One doesn't have to "live there" to know that one wouldn't *want* to live there if he or she were to become a victim of prejudice or malicious treatment.

I should note at this point that I suspect that such judgments of value across cultures are well grounded only in cases of what we might call "core" morality—that is, issues having to do with basic human rights and justice. Cross-cultural judgments about less basic issues, I would suggest, are more likely to be influenced by our own cultural bias. If I know, for example, that the citizens of another country halfway around the world are being arrested, tortured, and imprisoned without trial, I can reasonably judge this to be wrong—whether or not I happen to be a native of that country. On the other hand, I would be well advised to withhold judgment about, say, wedding customs in that country until I know more about why it is that such "odd" goings-on occur. Indeed, I may never be able to understand such practices, whereas I can fully empathize with the citizen of any country who is denied his or her basic human rights.

It should be noted at this point that a person can also judge his or her own culture and find it to be wanting in some regard. One usually focuses on a particular practice within a culture and not on the whole culture, of course, but one's own culture ought to come under careful scrutiny as well. It may be possible to argue that, "with respect to their treatment of the elderly, one culture is superior to another." But it is difficult to imagine how one would make blanket judgments about cultural superiority or inferiority, to say, for example, that one culture is superior in every way to another—any other. That way lies ethnocentrism, and that path is to be avoided. The surest way to avoid it is to admit that cross-cultural judgments cut both ways: they also apply from other cultural perspectives to one's own.

One might, for example, judge the traditional attitude of many Native Americans toward nature superior to that of white industrialists who see it as something simply to be exploited. This judgment can be made on utilitarian grounds in light of the distressing consequences that have followed on the heels of the "Protestant work ethic." That is to say, these judgments can be made *across* cultural boundaries about the values espoused in one culture from the perspective of another culture, regardless of which culture one happens to inhabit. The grounds for these judgments can be said, in principle, to transcend cultural boundaries because they are susceptible to acceptance or rejection by any rational person who takes the time and trouble to investigate the matter thoroughly. In this view, no culture is privileged, none is above rational scrutiny.

~

Cultural relativism is unacceptable for a variety of reasons. As mentioned above, the view insists that because a given culture regards an action as wrong, *therefore* it is wrong. This claim commits what G.E. Moore once called the "naturalistic fallacy" by concluding that an action *ought* to be judged wrong because it *is* judged wrong (in that culture). I shall elaborate on this point momentarily. Second, the view is contradictory. It advocates tolerance for all cultural values and simultaneously insists that everyone in every culture ought to agree—that is, it will not tolerate dissent on this point. If tolerance is indeed a value, and it would certainly seem to be, then cultures that exhibit intolerance are wrong to do so. But the relativist cannot take this last step without maintaining that tolerance is *truly* valuable—that is, it ought to be recognized as valuable by everyone. Thus, the relativist cannot maintain a consistent position. Third, if values can be said to be the result of enculturation, we cannot explain how it is possible for someone who is raised within one culture to find grounds for criticism of his or her own cultural practices. This happens frequently and is an important part of cultural advancement and growth. I shall return to this point in a moment as well. Fourth, it is impossible to say precisely what culture a person belongs to since we all are members of a variety of subcultures and in some cases members of several cultures at the same time.

It is possible, for example, for a young woman to be a mother, a member of the PTA, a graduate of a prestigious eastern university, active in her church, a participant in a literary society, and a frequent traveler between New York and Paris—while speaking both English and French fluently. Which cultural attitude, precisely, is she supposed to reflect? In fact, if we allow that enculturation occurs (as, indeed, it does), then it would seem that this woman is a product of many cultural attitudes, some of which conflict with one another and all of which she must assimilate and order by means of "cross-cultural" judgments.

Cultural relativists must defend the status quo and cannot explain how it is possible for a culture to develop a broader or more enlightened perspective. Indeed, they cannot account for change. The cultural relativist cannot explain the phenomenon of a Socrates, Christ, or Buddha who takes a stand against his own culture and adopts attitudes that were previously unknown. Socrates, for example, held that it is wrong to harm one's enemies as well as one's friends because, in doing so, one harms oneself to a much greater extent. This claim followed from Socrates's convictions about the nature of the human soul and the need for inner harmony and balance. So far as we know, this view had not previously been held in Athens, which tended to regard justice as a matter of helping one's friends and harming one's enemies. It was an attitude that was certainly not widely shared even among Socrates's friends. In addition, Plato held that women could rule his republic as philosopher kings. This view was radical in his day and was immediately rejected by subsequent thinkers. Christ repeatedly attacked the rigid moral and legal priestly order, as when he stopped the stoning of an adulteress. One can find numerous examples that cannot be explained in the narrow terms of relativism.

To expand upon a point above, made in passing, if we view cultural relativism systematically, we find that the view rests on an unwarranted assumption—namely, that "the values espoused by a given culture are the values that *ought* to be espoused by that culture." As noted, this view involves a confusion between the descriptive and the normative—to wit, "the naturalistic fallacy." Awareness of the fallacy goes back to Hume, who argued that one cannot infer "an *ought* from an *is,*" and as mentioned, was elaborated by G.E. Moore in 1907. Indeed, cultural relativism collapses the distinction between what is valued and what ought to be valued and ignores the latter altogether. What this means is that the relativist is reduced to resting moral claims on whimsy and adjudicating differences by means of force or intimidation. This unfortunate aspect of cultural relativism follows from the reduction of all standards of evaluation to cultural standards and the concomitant refusal to allow for the possibility of standards outside a given culture, which may in no way depend upon the views held within that culture.

In a word, one cannot explain value claims on the grounds that values and our reasons for holding those values are simply handed to us by those who raised us. To be sure, enculturation does occur, but each of us is more than merely a product of a given culture: at the very least, as suggested above, we are products of multiple cultures and subcultures. Furthermore, as humans who can reason, we are able to examine and lay bare the grounds of our value judgments and disclose them as defensible or unfounded. If they rest on error, confusion, bias, narrowness of vision, or sheer stupidity (which are all human characteristics), then they are groundless and ought to be abandoned. That we are unwilling to abandon our views in a particular case, even though we know them to be on weak grounds, is also a human foible. But it has nothing to do with our present concern.

At every turn, however, we are admonished not to be "judgmental," and when we dare to be so, we are asked,

"Who's to say?" The answer is that *anyone* can "say" if he or she is willing and able to grasp values and provide reasonable support for the value judgments made. The popular notion that one ought not to be judgmental is itself, of course, judgmental, but it is appropriate only in simple cases of self-regarding actions and such things as eating cake and the aesthetics of home decorating. In more complex cases, those which I called "core" morality above, it makes perfect sense to form value judgments and to seek to back them up—especially if the objects or actions being evaluated are of serious import and have consequences that affect others. As mentioned above, for example, it is not plausible to question such frivolous things as the wedding customs in a foreign country; however, it makes perfect sense to condemn injustice, wherever it is found. I will also argue in the next chapter that it makes sense to attempt to select from the mass of publications that flood our bookstores those worthy of serious attention and study. One cannot avoid being "judgmental." The admonition not to be so makes sense only with regard to frivolous comparisons.

The kernel of truth behind the admonition not to be "judgmental" is that everyone and everything have some worth when viewed dispassionately, and one ought to tolerate differences that make no difference. But it is absurd to rule out of court judgments that lead to those important discriminations and comparisons that are required to make informed choices.

⌒

There is a final consideration that must be weighed before closing this discussion. The cultural relativist, or the cultural anthropologist, makes the seemingly unarguable claim that behavior differs widely from one culture to another. Oddly, this variety is often exaggerated. I also suspect it is misperceived. Let us take an example.

I mentioned above the different practices between two cultures with regard to treatment of the elderly. On the face of it, we have two widely divergent practices that seem to reflect widely divergent values. One culture, for example, might be the native people who were encountered by the early explorers of the Hudson Bay. These men were shocked when they saw the natives killing their parents when they could no longer contribute to the tribe. Upon examination, it was discovered that the natives believed that, when they died, they would be reborn in the same condition they were in at death. Old people *wanted* to die before they became senile. Now if the second culture is the culture of the explorers themselves, it is quite possible that although they revered the elderly and tried to keep them home to help raise their children, their *reasons* for treating the elderly that way were precisely the same as the *reasons* the native people killed their elderly: in both cases, the elderly were treated with respect and affection—as the younger people would want to be treated when they, too, became elderly. In a word, differences may not be as extreme as they appear at first sight, and one of the main arguments of cultural relativism weakens upon careful scrutiny. Actions that appear different may be engaged in for the same reasons or in the name of the same principles. That is, actions may differ, but values may not: the differences may be merely apparent. Values may be more widely shared than they appear to be at first glance.

The only reasonable approach to the resolution of moral conflicts across cultural boundaries is within the framework of the *human* community. In this regard, differences are less interesting than similarities, and the major similarity is that all humans espouse values; have the capacity to love, to experience pain, and to reason; and are *therefore* worthy of respect.

The fundamental flaw in cultural relativism, then, is that it confuses a part of the truth for the whole truth: persons are affected by cultural influences, and value judgments often conflict with one another. But persons, because they are capable of reasoning, can rise above these factors and make sound judgments based on facts, valid argument, and ultimately, an appeal to the values themselves—as we shall see in the next chapter. Accordingly, it is possible to resolve moral conflict—at least in principle.

Chapter 4

What Are Values?

Value dwells not in particular will.
It holds his estimate and dignity as well
wherein 'tis precious of itself as in the prizer.
                    —William Shakespeare

Ironies and puzzles abound at the center of much of post-modern thought. It is ironic, for instance, that postmodernists react violently to the shortcomings of modernism and reject "technoscience" as too restrictive and unyielding to novel ways of knowing, only to adopt an equally exclusive paradigm of their own that rules out anything that smacks of "enlightenment" mentality. The "despised logos" can find no room at the postmodern table, which gives every appearance of being a disordered smorgasbord.

It is also ironic that despite their intense hatred and suspicion of science, postmodernists have adopted a positivistic attitude toward values, an attitude that recognizes only observable, scientific evidence and rejects all other forms of knowledge. As it happens, this is in keeping with a trend in the twentieth century that arises from, among other things, the growth of the social sciences and their tendency to mimic the value-free paradigm of the natural sciences. Consequently, as we have seen, values have generally come to be regarded in the popular mind as nothing more than personal feelings and, as such, unworthy of serious attention: after all, value judgments cannot be verified by scientific experiments. In order to avoid the reduction of values to feelings, Gertrude Himmelfarb recently proposed that we begin to discuss "virtues" instead and avoid the use of the word *value* altogether (Himmelfarb 1995). I would suggest, rather, that we seek a better grasp of the nature of values before we abandon the term entirely. That will be the focus of the present chapter.

Values, I shall argue, are relational properties that make up a portion of complex wholes that have an objective as well as a subjective aspect. They cannot be reduced to valuation without leaving a residue, and this residue is an essential part of what we mean when we talk about values. To be sure, there is a subjective response, which is what seems to receive all the attention these days; but there is also an objective aspect that consists of the properties of those wholes to which we respond. Reduction of value to evaluation results, inevitably, in subjectivism or relativism, because the objective aspect is ignored and the only thing left to talk about is our personal or culturally determined response. Worse still, since responses vary considerably even within a given culture, it is difficult to say which is a "better" or a "worse" response, and all count equally. This, of course, leaves us nowhere to turn when we attempt to resolve difficult conflicts.

I shall attempt to counter this popular view by carefully examining the ignored aspect of value judgments—namely, the values themselves. It is my contention that values are vital features of our everyday world, and relativism can be avoided by reference to the world we all share in common.

Values are experienced directly as qualities of objects or events. In art, for example, we find them in the region of properties that can be directly perceived—say, in that painting or this passage of Brahms's Second Symphony. For this reason, Monroe Beardsley called them "regional" properties. They can be found not only in art but elsewhere in the world as well, and they constitute the value and richness of human experience. They are also sometimes called "gestalt" qualities, and I shall use the terms *regional* and *gestalt* interchangeably—though, strictly speaking, the former term refers to the location of values, whereas the latter refers to their felt quality, or the way we experience them. Let us examine several examples to make clear what these properties are and how we happen upon them as we come and go.

If a musician completes a flawless performance of a Bach cantata or a ballerina performs an especially complicated pirouette with exceptional dexterity and breathtaking grace, we realize that we are in the presence of something extraordinary. This "something" is the complex of regional qualities that compose the event's value. Our capacity to react sensitively to these qualities is what Calvin O. Schrag called "discernment." He noted, in this regard, that "one discerns not only the truth of propositions, one also discerns the pain in the shriek, the love in the caress, the anger in the

shaking fist, the beautiful and sublime in the artist's creative work, the fitting response to the ethical dilemma, and
the proper conduct in a situation of social conflict" (Schrag
1992, 61). With this in mind, I would define *values* in the
following way:

> *"Values" are regional properties of objects or events
> that "require" a positive response on the part of any-
> one who considers the object or the event with dis-
> cernment.*

Before I proceed to explain this definition, I should mention what sorts of values I shall be considering in this study
and what sorts I shall ignore. There are many kinds of
values that fall into one of two major categories: *intrinsic*
or *extrinsic* values. The latter are those things that we consider valuable as a means to an end—such as, say, a match,
a hammer, or money—which are useful and therefore ex-
trinsically valuable. In this book, I am ignoring extrinsic
values, sometimes also referred to as "instrumental" values.
I am focusing my attention on intrinsic values, those aspects or features of our world that are valuable in themselves, whether or not they have any particular use.

I should note in passing that anything that has extrinsic
value can become intrinsically valuable if, for some reason,
our attention is drawn to the object itself—its regional qualities—rather than focused on the object from the perspective of utility. This can occur in cases of perversion—as
when the miser is fascinated with money for its own sake.
More interesting, for my purposes, is the case of the artist
who frequently creates art objects by transforming extrinsic

values into intrinsic ones. I shall explain this point later in the chapter.

In speaking of things that are valuable for their own sake, I prefer the term *inherent* to emphasize the fact that attention is on the qualities themselves that "require" positive responses. The relativist, of course, denies that anything can be inherently valuable. But I shall argue in this chapter that certain features or aspects of our common world are, indeed, inherently valuable. That is, they are capable of "requiring" a positive response—whether or not, in fact, anyone happens to be aware of them. Thus, the painting in the attic that everyone has forgotten is still valuable if, once it has been rediscovered, it can be shown that it exhibits features that "require" a positive response. The phrase "positive response" suggests a wide variety of responses that reflect our interest in the object or event—from simple approval to pleasure, joy, or delight. I shall try to make each of these points clearer as I proceed.

My definition seeks to establish the independent status of values as properties of objects and events in our common world that "require" positive responses. I place this term in quotation marks to distinguish this kind of requiredness from, say, the government requirement that we pay taxes. In contrast, we discern the "requiredness" of values in the way that we discern that $A > B$ and $B > C$ "requires" that we acknowledge that $A > C$. "Requiredness" is a gestalt quality described by Wolfgang Köhler in his book *The Place of Value in a World of Fact* as "the vector aspect of phenomenal objects," an aspect that "means that vectors issuing in parts of certain contexts extend beyond those parts and refer to other parts with a quality of acceptance or rejection. These other parts themselves assume the dependent properties of *right* or *wrong*. Whatever other differences there might be between logic, aesthetics and ethics—and there are important differences—this general trait seems to characterize requiredness everywhere" (Köhler 1959, 98).

This passage echoes Schrag's notion of "discernment," which suggests that it is the "requiredness" of values that discernment reveals. Schrag is interested in our reaction to value, whereas Köhler is interested in the values themselves. I share Köhler's interest in the values but wish to retain the notion of discernment as vital to our understanding of the way we respond to values. The doctrine may sound esoteric, but it is not. It is rather commonplace, as I shall show by means of several more examples.

If we are watching a tennis match with a trained tennis professional, it is quite likely that we will not be seeing the same match. If we start to discuss what we are watching, we may well discover that there are features or aspects of what is taking place (out there, on the court) that we had not previously seen. When one of the players hits an exceptional forehand winner down the line, for example, we aren't quite sure what happened, except that the player won the point. Indeed, we may not even see why it should be regarded as an "exceptional" shot. The professional, on the other hand, saw what was happening and was able to place the shot within a context that is both broad and deep—made up of thousands of such shots, few of which were hit quite as well. If we have a video camera and TV set handy, perhaps we can see what happened in slow motion once it is pointed out to us, though it is doubtful, since we lack the expert's frame of reference. In any event, the professional saw everything at once, which is to say, he saw aspects or features of the event that we missed.

So also with a ballet master or a skating instructor who decides that her pupils need to practice that arabesque or the death spiral again because they haven't got it "quite right." In a concert performance, a musician with a sensitive ear can detect flaws and dissonances that most people in the audience do not hear. A casual walk in the woods with an expert birder will reveal facets of our world we had never before known existed. I have a colleague who is blind and can hear Fritz Kreisler switch from his fourth to his third finger when playing a particularly high note. In each case, there is something going on in our world that we hadn't noticed until someone else pointed it out to us.

The same phenomenon occurs when we look at a painting with a trained artist or when we judge ethical actions with an unbiased, sensitive, and experienced observer. It happens again and again when we read a novel after having read the comments of an astute critic. Others often do persuade us that things are happening, or features are present in objects, that we had not observed previously and that "require" a positive response.

At times, of course, it is possible that we *project* our feelings and expectations into the world—perhaps because we are swayed by the reputation of the critic, the expert, or the professional. It is also possible that we succumb to the power of persuasion. But much of the time, we discover features and aspects of our world we had previously missed. Even if we do not, we have no grounds for claiming they are not "there." I cannot hear Kreisler switching fingers on the high notes, but I have no doubt whatever that he does it.

To the extent that these features of everyday objects and events are phenomenally present and "require" positive responses, I call them "values." And our common world is replete with values, though we frequently fail to perceive them or we deny their presence when they are pointed out to us. In ethics, values often appear in the guise of "virtues," or qualities that exhibit themselves in the extraordinary actions of men and women. Let me close this portion of the chapter with an example of a moral virtue that "requires" our positive response when we note its presence.

You and I are walking near a stream swollen from yesterday's rain that is now a raging torrent. We witness a young man on the far bank throw off his shoes and leap into the water in pursuit of a small girl. The man grasps the girl, swims to shore, and resuscitates her. The girl struggles into consciousness and lets out a long, frightened, but very animated, cry. The young man, though clearly exhausted, smiles and lets out a deep sigh.

As we reflect on this incident later, we agree that what the man did was "courageous." He put his life at risk to save another: what he did was "right." Anyone doing precisely the same thing under the circumstances—even if the girl had not recovered—would also have exhibited courage. As we reflect, we realize that our approval is "required" in the sense of the term I have used in this discussion thus far. We find ourselves, perhaps, smiling along with the young man—and letting out a sigh of relief as well.

Value, in the form of courage, is as much a part of this

event as are the young man's shoes, his wet clothing, the look of relief on his face, or the girl's lively cry at the end. Furthermore, if others disagreed with our evaluation, we would insist that they were mistaken—they lack discernment, perhaps—just as we would if they claimed the man's clothing wasn't wet. The value judgment refers to a part, at least, of the actual event. It is a response to a feature of the event that is phenomenally objective.

"Requiredness" is a felt quality of experience; it is immediate and direct and cannot be deduced from some other quality or property, though it is related to them systemically, as I shall argue below. The conclusion of a logical syllogism (or an arithmetic equation), the resolution of the tensions generated in a musical phrase, and the appropriateness of a particular action "require" a positive response on our part: as Köhler notes, it is what logic, aesthetics, and ethics have in common. Furthermore, the response is not arbitrary, nor is it merely personal, though each of us assuredly experiences it in our own way. It is controlled by the qualities in the object or the event. Readers familiar with the ontology of Charles Peirce will recognize in "requiredness" Peirce's description of our reaction to what he calls "firstness," the "quality-element of experience," which is felt rather than inferred (Peirce 1955, 87).

~

In order to show how we can become aware of those features of objects or events that "require" a positive response, I would like to suggest a systemic model. I shall take the case of a situation or an event that is composed of features or aspects that are related to one another and to the spectator as parts of a whole "system." Take the rather simple case of an extrinsic value, an object (in this case, coal) that has a degree of usefulness: when burned, it can keep our home warm. I shall argue from this simple case to an analogous case of the intrinsic value of courage, mentioned above. This will enable me to show how the systemic relationship of values to one another and to neutral, or value-free, properties of events and objects can help us to become aware of the presence of values when it is in doubt.

Suppose that, in situation U, there are no persons present but coal is present. In U, coal has value because *if* persons were present in U who did use the coal, it would turn out to have certain predictable and beneficial effects (it would provide heat) and therefore "require" a positive response from the user. Also, because these beneficial effects are related to one another, to the evaluator, and to the value of the coal systemically (that is, as parts of the same complex system), the evaluator can increase the likelihood of his or her awareness of the value of the coal by becoming aware of its benefits and the relationship of these benefits to other features of situation U. The coal is lighted, it glows and provides a warmth that we can experience, and our discomfort is alleviated: we feel warmer, and it pleases us. In a word, we can reflect on the features of situation U as they are related to one another, and to ourselves as beneficiaries of the coal-when-burned, to increase the likelihood of our awareness of the use-value of the coal itself. One does not simply stare at the coal waiting for it to exhibit its usefulness!

By analogy, in situation C, certain people behave in certain ways—a young man jumps into a raging stream to save a drowning girl—and we say that courage is a part of C for the following reasons: (1) were there another situation, C′, in which the young man did *not* jump into the water to save the girl, and the girl drowned, we would say of C′ that several of the phenomenally objective features of the situation that "require" our positive response are absent whereas they are present in C, and (2) were there a comparable situation, C″, in which a young girl's life were saved, then certain valuable results would occur in C″ as they did in C (panic is eliminated, fear reduced, self-esteem increased, a life saved, etc.), and these results indicate the presence in both C and C″ of the value of courage. The presence of value in systems such as C or C″ is indicated by the presence in those systems of other values (in parentheses above) as well as certain descriptive features of the event: the river was a torrent, the girl was in a panic, order was restored, the young man was exhausted, people smiled and evidenced relief, and so forth.

If we disagree about the presence or absence of value in a situation, what we typically do is consider the situation, and other situations of that type, in terms of those features related to one another as parts of the same system or complex, in an attempt to determine whether or not the value is present, that is, whether that event exhibits one or more features that should "require" a positive response. Reason is assisted by an affective/intuitive response to the "requiredness" of the values present in the situation, which Schrag aptly called "discernment."

We become aware of specific features of situations and events by becoming aware of other, related features of those situations or events. Courage is a value in situation C (as it is in C″) *because* its presence in C saved a life, increased self-esteem, and reduced fear and pain, just as its absence would *not* have produced those results. More to the point, it is a value because its presence "requires" our approval.

My definition of value suggests that values are regional properties of objects and events, which is not to say that their status is not in some way dependent upon the evaluator. I have also said that values are relational and part of a "transaction." But total dependence on the subject is not plausible, because values are *discerned* as features or qualities of our everyday world that elicit positive responses. In this view, response is a necessary condition of values, but it is not sufficient. Feelings are no more what values are all about than values that are ignored are fully values. Let me be clear about this.

The qualities we come to value are putatively "there" in the object or the event, dormant and waiting to be experienced— the tones of the melody that need to be heard to become a harmony, the colors on the canvas that need to be seen to be recognized as complementary, the sculpture on the pedestal that needs to be circled in order to be appreciated as graceful and elegant, or the relief on the young man's face as the girl recovers that needs to be witnessed or recounted to elicit joy in the spectator. Values are properties of objects and events in the real world, but their presence is discerned only if we assume the appropriate standpoint and adopt the appropriate attitude. This requires sensitivity, imagination, and cognition on the part of a spectator: the existence of values depends, as mentioned, on a "transaction" between subject and object. Because of the necessary involvement of a subject in the presence of value and the felt quality of value experience, many have tended to ignore those qualities of objects and events "out there" that trigger our responses; they therefore reduce values to evaluation. But we do not create values, strictly speaking; we discover them.

~

The view defended here has been called both "axiological realism" and "objectivism." It must be carefully distinguished from an absolutistic view that regards values as fixed and immutable, unchanging features of static objects. On the contrary, I would insist that we must take context into account—at least when it comes to evaluation—and acknowledge that the subject who makes the judgment is never the same person twice over: she brings different baggage to the discussion at different times. This is the element of truth in the relativistic position. However, these relative factors can be taken into account without admitting that value judgments are *reducible* to those factors.

John Hospers has shown convincingly how context relates to the manner in which we grasp aesthetic values. He argues against general norms and standards in aesthetic criticism while emphasizing the objectivity of the values we do grasp contextually. Probably the most convincing example he uses is a brief passage from *King Lear* in which

> Lear is dying near the dead body of his one faithful daughter Cordelia. His last words are
>
> [N]o, no, no life!
> why should a dog, a horse, a rat have life

And thou no breath at all? Thoul't come no more,
Never, never, never, never, never!
Pray you, undo this button: thank you, sir.
Do you see this? Look on her, her lips.
Look there, look there!

(Act V, Scene 3)

As Hospers points out, "it would be quite impermissible [as a rule] to have a line of poetry consisting of 'never' repeated five times ... yet in this context ... it achieves incandescence" (Hospers 1982, 328).

The importance of context cannot be overstated. It is what I was alluding to earlier in this chapter when I suggested the notion of the "systemic" relationship among the qualities or features of events and objects that allows us to become aware of certain features (such as values) by becoming aware of others. This does not mean that because a feature "works" in one context it is *always* valuable. Such an inference is unwarranted and one I would not make. My claim is that *if* a feature of an object or an event is valuable, *then* it "requires" a positive response by all who consider it carefully. The same feature in another context might not "require" any response whatever: it might not work in that context.

～

The standard objection to axiological realism, however, is that if value is present in events and objects—it is not simply a fiction, something we imagine or project into the world after it has been suggested by someone we admire or respect—then why don't more people agree about what is valuable? Why is there so much disagreement in ethics and aesthetics?

What we are faced with at this point are really two separate issues. First, there is the matter of widespread disagreement, which is a simple question of fact, and second, there is the question of the *basis* for the claim that values are present in the world. Let us take the first issue, since it is more easily disposed of.

The fact that people agree or disagree about values or that disagreement is prevalent (though this point is usually exaggerated) is beside the point. Agreement or disagreement proves nothing about the validity of a claim under debate. Whether or not the claim "Robins are larger than wrens" is true depends in no way whatever upon our agreement or disagreement in this case. We may agree, or we may not: it doesn't affect the truth of the claim. The axiological realist would simply maintain that *if* the claim is true, *then* we should all agree, in principle. There are many reasons why we may not agree, but these are all irrelevant to the issue. The same holds for value judgments, which is why my definition includes the term *require* in quotation marks: it is not always the case that people respond to the "requiredness" of values in the way they should (all things being equal).

With this in mind, what basis is there for holding that values are indeed independent features of our common world? It will not do to say that those who do not respond to the requiredness of values are inattentive or that they are stupid, boorish, insensitive, or prejudiced—though some or all of these things may be true. The basis for the claim is, rather, that its denial doesn't make any sense. We cannot account for the fact (uncommon though it may be) that we occasionally *agree* about values except by positing something "out there" about which we come to agree.

One might insist that agreement is simply a coincidence. But this is a bit of a stretch, since agreement always seems directed toward the object: it is *that painting* we come to agree is well done or *that action* we come to agree was, indeed, courageous. And we come to agree with one another after we have talked about it in great detail—even though we disagreed at first and may hate the idea of agreeing with one another.

~

As previously mentioned, at times, it is difficult, if not impossible, to tell whether a spectator is experiencing qualities of the object or merely projecting his or her own personal sensibilities onto that object. This does not mean that it can *never* be determined whether or not the spectator is projecting or responding appropriately to the object; it means that there are borderline cases in which it is admittedly difficult. One such case was discussed recently in an issue of *B.B.C. Music* that focused on the controversy in England over the admission of girls to Anglican church choirs. A careful look at this example will prove instructive.

Some experts, such as Richard Seal of Salisbury Cathedral, insisted that there is a qualitative difference between the voices of young girls and young boys and that the two were "separate acts of creation and best heard separately" (*B.B.C. Music* 1996, 19). He was quite specific in noting that "boys sing with a slightly heavier sound . . . more focused, able to provide pinpoint accuracy. Girls' voices are lighter in texture, more transparent, less able to match the men" (*B.B.C. Music* 1996, 19). His language suggests that Seal heard *something,* and organist Anthony Crossland tended to agree with him. But several other experts, such as Barry Rose, formerly in charge of music at St. Paul's and Canterbury Cathedrals, insisted that "the only difference between the sexes may come as a boy's voice moves toward breaking—there's a flowering of the sound that is very special, very distinctive" (*B.B.C. Music* 1996, 20). James Whitbourn, another expert with impeccable credentials, tended to agree with Rose but went even further in denying any real difference in sound. Who is correct in this controversy? It is tempting to assume that Seal and Crossland are simply imagining things. But the more interesting assumption is that they have heard a real difference between the quality of the boys' and the girls' voices. It is more interesting, because it leads to further questions. Furthermore, we should hesitate to dismiss the testimony of such people as Seal and Crossland, because they might be correct. In the case of my blind friend who can hear when Fritz Kreisler switches from his fourth to his third finger to play the high notes on his violin, am I to assume that he is merely imagining things, or must I assume that his hearing is simply more acute than mine? I strongly suggest the latter is the case.

In any event, I would take the stand that one or the other party to this quarrel is mistaken, and both might be. I argue that the quarrel can be settled, in principle, by careful listening, though in cases such as these, a resolution may be difficult to reach as a matter of fact. The relativist, on the other hand, would dismiss the entire controversy as bogus and would insist that there is no right or wrong, there are simply different ways of hearing and no way, in principle, to reconcile apparent differences. One must admit that, in cases such as this, a resolution may fall through what Monroe Beardsley called "the wide mesh of critical argument" and end up in the "Area of Rational Undecidability" (Beardsley 1958, 536). What is not clear, however, is that we should abandon every attempt to resolve this and similar issues simply because they are disputes about values and "therefore" insolvable. But that is precisely what the relativist would have us do.

In the end, this particular controversy may well have been resolved, for all practical purposes, when Graham Forbes, provost of St. Mary's Cathedral in Edinburgh, conducted the following experiment. He arranged to have "boys and girls choirs sing behind a screen to delegates at a national organists' conference—individually and in various combinations of voices." The results were that the delegates were unable to discern any noticeable difference between the boys' voices and the girls'. The group "scored no better than if they'd simply pulled the answers out of a hat" (*B.B.C. Music* 1996, 20). The boys and girls in these choirs, be it noted, had been trained together, and the conclusion reached was that whatever differences there might be between the voices of young boys and young girls were due to training and were not inherent in the groups. The experiment suggests, then, that Seal and Crossland did, in fact, detect a difference between the voices in question but that this difference was accidental and not endemic. To be sure, the experiment does not settle the matter once and for all, but it points the way to a reasonable solution—namely, to make the same training available to boys and girls. It also suggests that values are objective. One cannot claim that the point has been "proved," however.

What this controversy shows is not that spectators never project their own expectations onto the objects they experience but that, when a difference of opinion surfaces, appeal should be made to the world we share in common—though this appeal may leave the matter unsettled in a particular case. The "mesh of critical argument" is not fine, it is wide, as Beardsley noted. Furthermore, it "leaves a realm where rational argument does not reach, and where choice, if choice occurs, cannot be guided by reasons" (Beardsley 1958, 536). One should not infer, however, that we should therefore abandon all reasonable approaches to a solution. Such a conclusion is hasty and unwarranted, especially since these methods often take us a long way in the direction of a solution.

Judgments of value are corroborated by appeal to intersubjective experience, the world we share. There is no question of "privileging the self," as some writers have recently suggested; there is only the question of finding a reasonable way, through goodwill and the give-and-take of genuine dialogue to try to resolve conflict and adjudicate differences. This can be done only if we agree at the outset that conflict *can* be resolved reasonably by reference to a world of objective values. The process involves an openness to the world and a willingness to admit that we may be wrong.

We must be wary of making generalizations about values, however. They are difficult, if not impossible, to substantiate. Thus, I would insist that a claim such as "Brutus was wrong to have killed Caesar" is either true or false (it cannot be both). But I would hesitate to claim that "Killing is always wrong." This latter claim smacks of absolutism, which I have pointedly rejected. We can, if we wish, arrange values in some sort of crude hierarchy, though a commitment to a rigid hierarchy of values, once again, suggests absolutism. We do this regularly, however, when we urge students to take literature courses rather than basket weaving (because we think the former are more valuable, presumably), or when we assert that courage is better than amiability, or that saving the environment is more important than saving jobs. Even such generalizations, however, are questionable, because one can imagine a context in which the relationship will not hold. As mentioned above, my view holds that context is central to the experience of the worth of a value, though I would deny that it can *determine* the worth of that value. I shall argue this point carefully in the next chapter.

Because we must always work through the mist of our own prejudice and personal "economies," our grasp of values is never total or complete. The values are present in the world, but as Schrag has noted, this presence can be partial; that is, we "can speak of degrees of presentation, a contingent presence, which in our finite experience remains variable, partial, and incomplete—but which is an encountered presence nonetheless" (Schrag 1992, 97). Our *sense* of what things are truly valuable is never absolute. The objectivity of values in our world is therefore always a matter of degree.

~~

There are two threads to my argument that must be tied together to make a strong case against the reduction of values to subjective responses. On the one hand, I speak about values that are "phenomenally objective" features of our world. On the other hand, I speak about value *judgments* that are (presumably) about those features and that I insist are also objective. This second type of objectivity has to do with our knowledge of values; the former has to do with the values themselves. How are the two related?

If we claim that our value judgments are objective, we mean that they can be verified by anybody at any time. Karl Popper defined this type of objectivity rather nicely when he said that claims are "objective [when they are] *justifiable,* independent of anybody's whim: a justification [in turn] is 'objective' if in principle it can be tested and understood by anybody. [T]he *objectivity* of scientific statements [for example] lies in the fact that they can be *intersubjectively tested* " (Popper 1968, 44; italics in original).

Verification, or what Popper calls "justification," of claims, including value claims, is a function of argument support, coherence with other generally accepted claims, and appeal to features of our common world. If I am correct about values being phenomenally objective, then value judgments must ultimately refer to those features of our common world that provide the basis for correct value judgments. We saw this in our previous examples, in which argument support and evidence merge together to put us into a position to attend to the values present in the courageous act, the tennis match, and the skating competition.

The difficulty with value judgments is that the subjective elements tend to predominate: we generally care a great deal about acts of courage and great works of art—even about tennis and skating! Most of us don't have such strong feelings about Snell's law and chemical combustion. This, coupled with the mathematical evidence available in science, accounts for the greater degree of objectivity that attaches itself to scientific judgments as contrasted with value judgments—though we should be careful not to exaggerate the degree of objectivity of scientific statements. Even the most straightforward observations presuppose a theoretical framework that involves value judgments. I shall discuss this in a moment. For now, I would point out that the differences have most often dwarfed the similarities between value judgments and the perceptual judgments that abound in science, similarities that must also be acknowledged.

Justification in ethics and aesthetics, as Popper has noted, is not altogether different from verification in science. Bearing in mind that the objectivity of knowledge claims is a function of independence, we can safely say that the objectivity of scientific judgments is greater than that of value judgments, but the difference is one of degree, not kind.

Although we may, in point of fact, find it difficult to locate a particular judgment—be it one in science or in ethics—on the spectrum between the most subjective and the most objective (and perhaps even to find paradigm cases of objective and subjective judgments), I would nevertheless insist that objectivity is possible in ethics as it is in science, and for many of the same reasons. Subjective elements (bias, superstition, fear, ignorance, etc.) enter into practically every judgment we make. The more "objective" of these judgments are those in which the subjective elements have been eliminated through critical examination and discussion. But just as they can be eliminated in science, they can also be eliminated—with less success, unfortunately—in ethics. In this regard, Arthur Koestler noted that "there is certainly a considerable difference, in precision and objectivity, between the methods of judging a theorem in physics and a work of art. But I wish to stress . . . that there are continuous transitions between the two" (Koestler 1964, 330).

It might be interesting to go through each of the different sciences to examine the degree of objectivity that attaches itself to various claims. The same could be said of the claims made within a given science. For my purposes, however, this is not required. I need only note that the scientific method focuses attention on *inter*subjective verification and what Popper called "critical rationalism" to guarantee that the claims of science can be tested and warranted by anyone at any time and in any place. This is what guarantees the objectivity of those claims. The same thing is true, to a lesser degree, in the social sciences, which also "ground conclusions on reason and evidence of some sort" and are therefore both "rigorous and analytical" (Rosenau 1992, 168).

The ideal of total objectivity is achieved, if it is achieved at all, only in mathematics and logic. As we distance ourselves from this ideal, we find ourselves dealing with ever-increasing bias, prejudice, and narrowness of vision. This is true even for the most "exact" of the sciences, as Michael Polanyi has convincingly argued. As we move from the natural to the social sciences, of course, we move from greater to lesser objectivity—even though the social sciences have tended to mimic the natural sciences in their use of mathematics (usually in the form of statistics). What keeps the social sciences from wallowing in subjectivism is precisely the level of success they obtain in adapting the paradigm of the natural sciences, which is to say, their success in establishing their claims on grounds open to intersubjective verification and rational criticism. There are signs that postmodern thinkers within the social sciences have recently called this paradigm into question, and thinkers such as Pauline Marie Rosenau evidence concern about the effects of this sort of criticism on the future of social science.

Generally speaking, judgments of ordinary perception—within and without the social and natural sciences—can be considered objective to the extent that they involve claims that can (1) be verified by the claimant himself or herself at a later time, (2) be verified by people other than the claimant, or (3) withstand sustained criticism. This last consideration is most important because it is one that is available in the domain of value judgments. It is the heart of the Socratic "maieutic," and Karl Popper insists, rightly, that it is integral to the scientific method.

Rational criticism builds our confidence in value judgments; it may lead us to reject, modify, or adapt them in light of subsequent consideration. Throughout, we insist that agreement is possible, in principle if not in fact. It is not necessary to abandon the ideal of objectivity altogether in questions of values as though it were an impossible, and therefore useless, goal.

What we must do, then, is locate, identify, acknowledge, and (if possible) eliminate the subjective elements that obtrude in our judgments of value. For example, if I know that I cannot reason dispassionately about homosexuality because I am homophobic, my awareness of my own prejudices will help me to become better able to think about those issues—or make me realize that I must discount my own judgments as biased and not worthy of serious consideration by others. If I am a neo-Nazi, my evaluations of the worth of the man Hitler are suspect—to say the least. The relativists argue, in effect, that we are all homophobic or neo-Nazis (or something equally unpleasant) on every issue whatever involving values. This borders on the peculiar.

Furthermore, relativism—in any of its classical, modern, or postmodern guises—would insist that the project of eliminating personal prejudice and cultural bias is a futile hope. On the other hand, the view I am defending here would insist that it can be a fruitful enterprise, that value judgments are capable of being justified through argument, criticism, and the weighing of evidence—which includes relevant factual evidence coupled with the evidence provided by the values themselves. Whatever degree of objectivity we might be able to achieve through the use of these methods can be achieved by anyone at any time by adopting these same methods. Our success (or failure) is tested by our patience, openness, intelligence, sensitivity, and experience, that is, our discernment. Clearly, we often fail this test.

~~~

In defense of values, then, I would insist that there are objective as well as subjective aspects in value judgments. Further, I would insist that the objective aspects should not be ignored in favor of "individual economies." These are clearly present, but they do not *necessarily* exhaust every situation involving values—though they might in a given case. Value judgments are claims, and they can be justified reasonably. Ultimately, evidence for those claims must come from the values that are experienced directly as features of our common world. This is how the two threads of my argument must be tied together: the truth of value judgments is supported by evidence that will eventually draw our attention toward aspects or features of our common world that are phenomenally objective.

Chapter 5

Values in the Arts

*In all judgments by which we describe anything as
beautiful, we allow no one to be of another opinion,
not . . . that everyone will agree . . . but that he ought.*
—Immanuel Kant

One might think that aesthetics is a field in which, of all
places, theorists would be likely to resist the trend toward
value relativism. Such is not the case, however, as a cursory
glance at any current publications list in the field will reveal. Art theory has become another arena in which personal opinions reign supreme and expertise is viewed as
"privileging the self." With the exception of isolated thinkers such as Monroe Beardsley and Eliseo Vivas and, more
recently, Marcia Eaton—whom I shall consider in a moment—very few aestheticians have had much to say about
values at all. This is especially odd, since values abound in
the fine arts and, as I shall argue, extraordinary values constitute the greatness of certain works of art and literature. I
shall expound on this theme in this chapter and the next.

Colors, shapes, sounds, movement, and values are everywhere. They surround us, and they make up a part of what we call the world of human experience. Unlike colors and shapes, to which we can point, however, many people deny that values are "there" and insist that they are nothing more than a reflection of the way we experience the world. However, we do not *see* love or fear, hatred, and jealousy, but we do not deny their reality. Neither do we *see* the utility of the match. It is there nonetheless, and we realize it when we strike it and ignite the kindling on a cold day. We do not *see* the honesty of the young woman who gives the ten-dollar bill back to the old man who dropped it on the sidewalk. But it is an integral part of that situation as well.

Values are a part of the furniture of the world. That is my theme. Their presence is experienced directly in the "requiredness" that attends every value, and its presence can be confirmed by analysis, inference, and attention to the relationships between the basic elements that make up our experience. Our awareness of values is primarily a matter of feeling, but it is assisted by imagination and reflection. In his *Critique of Judgment,* Kant characterized judgments of "taste" as judgments based on feeling in which imagination and understanding tend to harmonize with each other. Calvin Schrag's notion of "discernment," as noted in the last chapter, suggests this complexity as well.

Values must be engaged fully in order to be fully realized as values. For example, I can be standing next to an art critic in a gallery who points out to me all the subtleties and nuances of the painting on the wall in front of us. I can acknowledge what she says and come to appreciate the painting intellectually and imaginatively. But unless the painting touches me, unless I respond fully to the "requiredness" of the values in the painting and am moved by it, I cannot be said to appreciate its value as a work of art. "Requiredness" must be experienced directly as a felt quality of experience and not merely inferred. Imagination and thought may be necessary, but they are certainly not sufficient to enable us to experience value—though they can prepare us, open us up as it were, to the "requiredness" of values that we experience directly. In the end, we value the painting because it is valu-*able:* the regional properties in the painting itself have the *capacity* to evoke a positive response and require me to value it as a work of art. When I judge a painting to be beautiful, for example, "the tribute seems to be wrung from me by the object" (Jessop 1969, 275).

In ethics, we find an interesting parallel. We witness an act of courage, and our response is a felt experience to the "requiredness" of the value that is present in the event. If we do not respond to the value, and we might not, a friend might be standing by who tries to make us aware of other features in the event that are related systemically to the properties we *should* find valuable. But unless we respond to the "requiredness" of the value itself, we cannot fully appreciate or acknowledge the action as one we *ought* to admire and emulate. After our friend points out the features of the event, we might well say, "Yes, I see what you're saying. The young man did risk his life, and the girl is now safe. But I still think it was a stupid thing for him to do. I'm not sure I would agree with you that he did the right thing." In saying this, we reveal our preoccupation with certain features in the experience to the exclusion of others.

If a person does not respond to values in the appropriate ways, then either of two things is true: (1) the person is not open to these qualities, for any number of reasons, or (2) the qualities are not phenomenally *there,* and re-examination is in order. What this means is that, as mentioned in the last chapter, judgments of value are corrigible, as is any judgment we make about our common world. The debate might go on, or it might stop there. But in any event, intellectual acknowledgment alone is not adequate: we must experience the "requiredness" of values directly and immediately in order to appreciate values fully.

Plutarch, for one, seemed convinced that this can occur, and that it often does, when he wrote his "parallel lives" of Greeks and Romans. Because virtue inspires and "requires" imitation, when we confront it directly and experience it fully, it is a fit subject for study. As he put it, "A colour, for example, is well suited to the eye if its bright and agreeable tones stimulate and refresh vision, and in the same way we ought to apply our intellectual vision to those models which inspire it to attain its own proper virtue through the sense of delight they arouse. . . . Moral good, in a word, has a power to attract toward itself. It is no sooner seen than it rouses the spectator to action . . ." (Plutarch 1992, 165).

In the arts, values are also "required," but we do not usually insist that people have a "duty" to espouse them, adopt them, or imitate them somehow. In responding to works of art, however, it makes perfectly good sense to say that one is "required" to have an appropriate response, usually in the form of aesthetic delight. We often say, for example, "You really ought to read this book. It's outstanding!" or "You should have heard the performance of the Brahms piano concerto the other night. It was superb!" The "ought" or "should" in these cases refers to the desire on the part of the speaker that the listener share a delightful experience, which will (presumably) be repeated for him or her as part of a later aesthetic experience. Values in the arts are no less public than values in ethics, though it is odd to speak about a "duty" to act a certain way in the company of art objects. This is because the values in the two cases are quite different.

We apprehend values in art objects in much the same way we do in ethics, however—by confronting the object, attending to it, and reflecting on the relationships between the parts of the whole object. Since *value* is another term for *excellence,* we might characterize the difference between ethics and the fine arts as having to do with two different sorts of excellence: in ethics, we are dealing with *human* excellence; in the fine arts we are dealing with the excellence of *objects,* which, though they are created by humans, are nonetheless still objects—be they paintings, compositions, works, or performances. To sharpen the focus somewhat, I would say that, as far as values are concerned, the chief difference between ethics and the fine arts is that, in the latter, the values we confront are aesthetic qualities of objects created by humans.

Aesthetic qualities are qualities of perceived objects that strike us immediately, without reflection. We not only see the silk as smooth or the velvet as soft; we can feel it without touching it. These are gestalt qualities that form an important part of the world we all experience. In a painting, for example, we might speak of the strong atmospheric quality or the vividness of the color red as set against the drab, colorless background. These are aesthetic qualities, and not only do they strike us immediately, but also they are often the qualities we recall later when we are thinking about the painting—just as we remember the face we saw yesterday as friendly or sad, even though we cannot quite describe it. These are what Beardsley called "regional" qualities, because they exist in the region of what he called the "local" qualities, which we can touch or point to. I mentioned the term *regional quality* briefly in the last chapter. It might be good to elaborate, in our present context, on the nature of these properties and how they contrast with "local" qualities.

In painting, colors, shapes, and lines are local qualities, which, when combined, give rise to such regional qualities as sensuousness, gleefulness, brightness, intensity, restlessness, boldness, playfulness, and mournfulness. It is these regional qualities that constitute the value that art objects have for us: these are the qualities that "require" a response that is typically joyful, delighted, or ecstatic.[1]

In the process of seriously engaging a work of art, such as a painting, we become aware of the regional qualities of the object. As we saw, these qualities contribute to the complex whole that is made up of elementary parts. They emerge from the various combinations of local qualities. As the gestalt psychologists are so fond of saying in this regard, the whole is more than the sum of the parts. In music, for example, Carroll Pratt has noted that

> when the notes *c* and *g* are sounded together they produce a quality which in music is called the Fifth. That quality is neither the *c* nor the *g*, nor does it depend on those particular notes. Any two tones with the ratio of $\frac{2}{3}$ will be immediately recognized as a Fifth no matter in what region of the scale they might be played. Fifthness is a Gestalt which is different

from either or any of its parts, and no amount of knowledge about the parts in isolation would ever give the remotest hint as to what Fifthness is like. (Köhler 1969, 10)

In painting, as an example, we can see how experts locate these qualities if we listen in on an author telling her readers how to look at Picasso's *Girl before a Mirror.*

> Unity is achieved in several ways, including the dominance of curved lines. The straight lines, horizontals and diagonals, serve as a kind of background "filler" to the large swooping curves, and they also provide linear variety. . . . The circle motif—be it face, breast, womb, or buttock—recurs in a rhythmic pattern. . . .
>
> Colors are brilliantly varied, but they fall generally in the same range of values and intensities, thus contributing to unity. A skeleton of dark, almost black values in shape and line, provides the structure on which the picture is "hung." . . .
>
> The balance . . . is predominantly symmetrical. Picasso has even provided a vertical line in the center of the composition to divide the two halves. Subtle differences between the girl's body and her mirror reflection enliven and relieve the symmetry. There is almost a pendulum effect as our eyes shift back and forth rhythmically between one side and the other—a pendulum effect enhanced by the curve of the arm.
>
> Finally . . . there is a figure eight rhythm that swoops us through the two figures. By introducing these rhythms Picasso has made what might have been a static image—a girl facing a mirror in a flat space—assume qualities of almost dancelike grace. (Gilbert 1992, 174)[2]

Note in this description the many regional qualities to which the author directs her readers' attention. She notes such qualities as the painting's "unity," its "swooping curves," its "linear variety," the "rhythmic patterns," the structure on which the picture is "hung," how subtle differences "enliven" and "relieve" the symmetry, the "pendulum effect," and of course, the "dancelike grace" of the images. These qualities cannot be pointed to, but our attention can be directed toward them, as it has in this case, by noting the relationships between these qualities and others to which the author *can* point and to which the regional qualities are related systemically.

But one might argue, evaluation is still subjective because one might acknowledge the local and even the regional qualities and still not experience aesthetic pleasure. Indeed, one might be "turned off" by this painting and even find it disgusting. This is true, of course, but it does not imply that evaluation is subjective: the spectator may lack discernment or, perhaps, have failed to adopt the aesthetic standpoint. Appreciation is difficult and requires imagination, close attention, and a willingness to open ourselves to what is happening on the canvas without bias or preconception. It also takes experience and some sophistication. In music, it requires a good ear and musical memory, which evidence suggests can be improved with experience. Without such a memory, the spectator cannot take in the whole musical performance and can only grasp the parts separately. In a word, we must attend to art the way we listen to music— as Vernon Lee noted some sixty-five years ago: "Listening, as opposed to simply hearing, [involves] the most active attention moving along every detail of composition and performance, taking in all the relations of sequences and combinations of sounds as regards pitch, intervals, modulations, rhythms, and coordinating them in a series of complex wholes, similar to that constituted by all the parts, large and small, of a piece of architecture . . ." (Lee 1933, 32).

In a word, the spectator must assume an active role in the transaction. But the evaluation does not depend upon the spectator's response alone. In the end, what he or she experiences are the values that emerge from the local qualities on the canvas or in the musical performance. And the local and regional qualities are objective—they are "really" there—or we have made a mistake and must look or listen again. The question can certainly be debated, but its resolution is only possible by reference to the art object. Responses, when they are appropriate, are not whimsical; they are controlled by the objects themselves. One more example might help to make this clear.

You and I are discussing the relative merits of musical compositions, and we decide to focus attention on a theme from Geminiani's Opus 3 and another from Bach's Prelude and Fugue for Organ (Meyer 1967, chap. 6). You argue that Bach's theme is far better, as is his fugue generally, because you find that Bach exhibits far greater control of his material, and the material itself involves delays and temporary diversions that heighten the suspense and satisfaction of the careful listener; it doesn't simply lead to a predetermined point as Geminiani's piece tends to do on the whole. That is to say, it is less predictable. Bach's piece exhibits greater diversity and variety and, in the end, provides considerably more musical information than does the selection from Geminiani. Bach's piece is more imaginative and far more astonishing and rewarding to the attentive listener; it bears repeated listening, whereas the other piece tends to become tiresome. As a result of these considerations, and others of a similar nature, you judge the Bach piece to be the *better* piece: it has more value because it tends to elicit a more positive response than does the Geminiani piece.

Whether or not your judgment in this case is *correct,* it is nonetheless plausible. More important, it is grounded in qualities or features of the music itself that are phenomenally objective. You are not simply projecting your subjective responses into the piece, as can be attested to by the fairly commonplace observation, mentioned in the last chapter, that I sometimes come to agree with you. Agreement sometimes arises not because I want to agree but because what you say makes sense and directs my attention to features of the piece I had not previously noticed.

Aesthetic values are most often found in art objects, though one can also find them in ordinary experience—the sudden flash of the emerald green on the mallard's head, the graceful movement of the doe as she leaps over the fallen tree and disappears into the woods, the brilliant sunset following the late afternoon thunderstorm, or even the graceful curve of the serving spoon at the dinner table, which we notice for the first time. As mentioned in the last chapter, these are examples of extrinsic values being transformed into intrinsic ones. This frequently happens when an artist creates a work of art. In this regard, we need to consider what an art object is.

⌣

This seemingly simple matter is, of course, immensely difficult. Over the years, aestheticians have offered a variety of responses to the question "What is art?" and they seldom

111

reach agreement. Once again, we can look to Monroe Beardsley for a suggestion that he made late in his long career as an aesthetician and a critic when he tried to take us beyond the obvious to a deeper understanding of what it is that makes the art object unique. He reasoned that an art object is one that is created by an artist with the intention of giving it the capacity to satisfy aesthetic interest (Curtler 1984, 21). Now, since an "aesthetic interest" is precisely what I have called a "positive response" to aesthetic values, Beardsley's definition of the art object would appear to offer great promise in the present context.

Note that Beardsley does not bother about whether or not the art object is "good" or "bad," only about whether it is an object of art. If Beardsley is correct, then, an art object is any object that the artist has made (or placed before us) with the intention of satisfying aesthetic interest. He or she can take an ordinary use-object and place it before us in a way that elicits aesthetic interest.

Since aesthetic interest is generated by aesthetic values, the question of whether or not an art object is any good depends upon the question of the kinds of value that one finds in the object. "Good" art is capable of generating intense and repeated delight, whereas "bad" art is not. Emphasis here must be on the *capacity* the object has to generate aesthetic interest, because it is immaterial whether or not it does so in fact. Beardsley was careful in his selection of this term. The failure of an art object to generate an aesthetic response may simply be the result of the spectator's failure to adopt the appropriate standpoint, as mentioned previously.

The point here is that "good" art embodies values, usually a great many, that "require" positive responses on the part of a discerning spectator. The multiplicity of the values present and their capacity to generate deep and frequent delight are characteristic of great art and allow us to understand the diverse and even conflicting responses to art that are commonplace. Different people respond differently to the host of values that are embodied in "good" or "great" art. This is no less true in the visual arts than it is in poetry and literature. I shall discuss literature more fully in the next chapter, but I will note in passing that it is, above all else, the multiplicity of values, in the form of possible meanings, in great literature that is a mark of its excellence: there are many more values to respond to in great literature than there are in literature of lesser status. This is why we return to great literature, and indeed to great art in general, again and again. The "language" of art—whether it be words, images, sounds, or properties of the object and the relationships of elements within the object to one another—grounds the object's values and generates the many possible meanings that complex objects have for us. In order to appreciate art, we must learn that language, because the way the artist chooses to communicate is a part of the value of the work as a whole.

Once again, we are brought back to the question of value. What are these values that the artist seeks to point out to us through his or her art? Let us approach this question obliquely. The territory will soon become familiar.

One of the more interesting attempts to define value in art in a way that calls attention to the objects themselves and not to our responses to those objects is that of philosophy professor Marcia Eaton. As she notes in this regard, "the *locus* of attention is the object when our delight is aesthetic and we recognize that the object is a necessary part of the *cause* of our pleasure" (Eaton 1988, 143; italics in original). Unfortunately, Eaton shows too much concern for the context in which art objects are encountered. As a result, she ends up in the lap of cultural relativism. It will be instructive to see how this happens in order to ensure that the definition I gave in the last chapter does not suffer the same fate.

Professor Eaton defines aesthetic value as "the value a thing or event has due to its capacity to evoke pleasure that is recognized as arising from features in the object traditionally considered worthy of attention and reflection" (Eaton 1988, 143). The pleasure is aesthetic pleasure, but I would still regard this as too narrow a term to include the many possible responses to aesthetic value—some of which are distinctly unpleasant, though still arguably "positive." Thus, the pain we feel in watching a performance of *The Women of Troy* is still positive in the sense that we learn and grow from it—and even want to repeat it. I have defined value in terms of this "positive response" to allow for a range of responses from pleasure to pain that arise from our encounters with art. I would thus reject this part of Eaton's definition as too narrow.

The main difficulty with this definition, however, arises from Eaton's insistence upon the place of tradition, not in our experience of art but in a definition of value. As she explains later in her text, "aesthetic value is objective to the extent that it depends on particular cultural traditions" (Eaton 1988, 145). To make the objectivity thus *depend* upon tradition is to reduce value to our experience of it as determined by our cultural traditions. Therefore, as mentioned, we are back once again in the lap of cultural relativism as I characterized it above.

Surely, we can allow for the relevance of tradition in determining the *presence* of values in an art object without making tradition a part of the values themselves. Indeed, it is difficult to know what this would mean. On its face, it is simply false. The value of a Ming vase or an African carving in no way depends upon the spectator's being Chinese or African. One can respond positively to values, even appreciate them, without being conditioned to do so by one's culture. But even if this were not the case, the value of the object does not depend upon the cultural tradition of the spectator who confronts it.

Eaton is stressing an important point, however. Even the gestalt theorists note the role of conditioning (tradition) in affecting response to such ordinary properties as physique ("She's beautiful!" or "He's homely.") and behavior ("Her action was exemplary!"). It is not clear, however, what, if any, gestalt qualities are due to cultural conditioning. The evidence suggests that such qualities as the warmth of the color orange and the sense that the color blue is retreating are universal. Furthermore, the open smile of a young child has a gestalt quality that is universally recognized—and differs from smiles that are sinister. So also in the case of the scowl, the look of fear or anguish, or the raised fist that Schrag mentions. These are all gestalt qualities, and as mentioned above in passing, the odd thing about them is that they are easier to remember than the qualities that give rise to them. In this regard, Carroll Pratt noted that "the friendliness of a face is more likely to be remembered than the width of the nose, the distance between the eyes, the part of the hair, the shape of the lips, the size of the ears, or even the color of the eyes" (Köhler 1969, 22).

It is not at all clear just what role tradition and conditioning play in the apprehension of these qualities. But to say that tradition is *essential* to the qualities themselves is not plausible. In a word, I might agree that tradition and conditioning play an important role in the way we respond to regional qualities in art, but they are not a determinant of value. They might help us to locate values, just as the context may assist us, but they cannot be said to be defining conditions of value, since neither is necessary nor sufficient. Whether or not an object has aesthetic values is determined, rather, by the presence or absence of regional qualities that "require" positive responses on the part of the attentive spectator. An unusual analogy may help me to make this point more clearly.

Take the case of a joke, even though humor is more subjective than art. If I can show that what is essential to the joke in no way depends on the tradition familiar to the person telling it or the one hearing it, it will be rather easy to make a similar point with respect to what is essential to value. Note the following example:

A. Have you heard that the library burned down at the local university?

B. No. Really?

A. Yes. It destroyed *both* books . . . and only one had been colored in!

As Arthur Koestler has shown, the humor arises when the listener or reader "gets" the joke, because of the bisociation between two independent "matrices" or frames of reference. The initial stage of the joke (A's first question above) sets up one frame of reference, within which the listener B responds as expected. The punch line then cuts across this frame of reference with suddenness and startles the listener. The tension built up (briefly) in the initial question is then released in the form of laughter. Or we may not laugh. It has no bearing on what makes the joke comical. Clearly, one's background, maturity, intelligence, and familiarity with the language will help to determine whether or not one laughs. But those things have nothing to do with the essential humor of the joke itself. Surely, *anyone* would show some concern upon hearing that a library had been burned down; and that person would not expect the response—whether or not he or she laughed. If the joke is comical, it is so because of bisociation: it has to do with the relationships between features of the joke—the "preamble" taken in conjunction with the punch line. In a word, the question of whether or not the joke is comical is separate from the question of whether or not we happened to laugh. The latter question has to do with "tradition"; the former does not.

There is a remarkable similarity in the case of value in art. Tradition, context, and conditioning play a part in our response to an art object (whether or not we "get it"), but they do not play a role in determining the place of value in the work. This is why I have placed the term *requiredness* in quotation marks throughout this discussion of value: one may respond positively to values, or one may not as a matter of fact. We can say (and we do, though we are reluctant to admit it) that one "ought" to respond to the "required-ness" of values—in ethics, to acknowledge them and to imitate them as well and, in aesthetics, to respond appropriately. This helps to explain why we are bothered, as Kant suggests in the comment quoted at the start of this chapter, when someone else doesn't like the book we recommended or turns away in disgust from a painting we particularly like. We want confirmation that our own responses are somehow legitimate, but we also feel that others *should* respond pretty much the same way we do.

Having come this far, can I pull some of the threads of this discussion together and begin to draw some tentative conclusions? I think I can.

An art object exists in the world: it is an object for a subject and exists in the transaction between the two. This means that it is objective and also that our experience constitutes it as an object for a subject. Consequently, it would be a mistake to reduce the art object to a thing in the world totally independent of any subject—such as the canvas on the wall, which is not identical with the art object *per se*—or to reduce it to mere subjective response, as with the popular view. The object is a complex nexus that grounds local and regional qualities that "require" a positive response—usually aesthetic delight. The qualities that generate delight

> make their appearance in art more often and more strikingly than anywhere else and are regarded by many authorities as the very essence of the tenacious hold that art has had in all

times and places. The music of Beethoven is often powerful and even titanic, although as in the case of Michelangelo's sculpture there are many examples of gentle tenderness; the faces of Renaissance madonnas are wistful and sad; the music of Mozart frequently is melancholy in spite of the gaiety of its surface; the glass of Chartres glistens with radiant color; many passages of Reger fairly burst with romantic fervor, etc. (Köhler 1969, 22)

❧

As traditionally conceived, art objects consist of a combination of "form" and "matter." I have ignored this distinction, because I am not convinced it helps us grasp the nature of aesthetic values and their relationship to art objects. Values seem to transcend this distinction, in that those properties that constitute values are neither simply form nor simply matter; they are both. One of the difficulties with this distinction is that it attempts to say what it is about *any* work of art that makes it "beautiful" or what kinds of things *always* make objects beautiful. I am not sure we can answer this question. As a general rule, I think it more productive in aesthetics—as in ethics, as mentioned in the last chapter —to concentrate attention on particular objects and ask what it is that makes *this* particular object generate a sense of delight. However, there may be one exception in art.

Unity does seem to be a particular regional quality that is present in every work of art. Whether or not this point be granted, a discussion of this particular regional quality will enable us to better grasp the unique character of artworks.

If, by *unity*, we mean that the work must be coherent or we refer to the inseparability of form from matter, or if we

119

mean to draw attention to the manner in which the artist has combined what she wanted to say with her manner of expression, then clearly unity is central to art. But art as art is fundamentally ambiguous, full of possible meanings, in the form of the many values that go to make it up. If we mean to suggest by our use of the term *unity* univocal meaning, then unity is not a part of the art object.

It is useful, however, to employ the term *unity* to draw attention to the distinctive character of artworks within which total satisfaction can be found and beyond which aesthetic attention does not tend to wander. This is certainly one of the major differences between works of art and other objects that surround us. Artworks are "autotelic"—that is, they demand that we attend to them alone, and (if they are any good) they capture and hold our attention in a tight grip and won't let it go. An example will show what I mean.

With due caution in the face of generalizations, I venture to say that Norman Rockwell's paintings are of lesser stature than any of the paintings of Rembrandt, Renoir, or Leonardo da Vinci, because Rockwell relied on the familiar and called forth sentimentality rather than sentiment. His works are formulaic and suffer from a lack of imagination and invention. His paintings are technically well done, but they lead inevitably beyond themselves: they are unable to hold the spectator's attention and imagination to themselves. Indeed, they seem designed to encourage reflection, fond recollections, and warm feelings of our childhood. Doubtless, this explains their popularity. Rockwell's art seldom if ever suggests a new way of seeing the world, and it always fails to exhibit real novelty. There is a sameness or monotony to his works that goes beyond questions of style to suggest a diminished imagination. In works that exhibit "greatness," on the other hand, one finds all that is missing in Rockwell, combined with technical skill and, above all else, genuine novelty. Take any painting of Renoir almost at random and it will hold one's attention and encourage exploration of the painting itself, as did Picasso's *Girl before the Mirror*. Afterward, we see our world differently, as was noted most eloquently by Marcel Proust some time ago:

> [T]he original painter, the original writer, proceeds along lines adopted by oculists. The course of treatment they give us by their painting or by their prose is not always agreeable to us. When it is at an end the operator says to us: "Now look!" And, lo and behold, the world around us (which was not created once and for all, but is created afresh as often as an original artist is born) appears to us entirely different from the old world, but perfectly clear. Women pass in the street, different from what they used to be, because they are Renoirs, those Renoir types which we persistently refused to see as women. . . . Such is the new and perishable universe which has just been created. It will last until the next geological catastrophe is precipitated by a new painter or writer of original talent. (Proust 1932, 1:950)

Without unity, it is not clear that art would have the power to effect this sort of response.

In painting, unity is brought about by the successful manipulation of all the complex elements that make it up. Design and composition combine with color, atmosphere, and the congruence of objects in space—all realized with consummate technical skill. Unity is not simplicity, it is a complexity that is ordered, marshaled to the artist's appointed ends.

If attention to the object flags and we ruminate instead of concentrating, then either the art is not very good or we are at fault. What I have called the "aesthetic standpoint" presupposes a number of conditions that must be fulfilled before we can say that the work has failed. I discussed this attitude above, but I should add a few more comments in closing this chapter.

As spectators, we must bring with us the correct frame of mind and leave unnecessary baggage at home—the prejudices and preconceptions we tend to carry around, together with inattention and unwillingness to open ourselves to something new and different. What we must bring, on the other hand, are elemental sensibilities, together with the capacity to attend to the work with sustained and concerted attention. In music, we must be able to detect pitch accurately and recall what has already been heard; in painting, we must be sensitive to color and be able to take in the work as a whole. These things are obvious, but they need to be stated. The spectator must develop his or her sensibilities as well through repeated exposure to works of art. Technical training in the art field in question would augment sensitivity to the regional qualities of the object, certainly. Knowledge of the tradition might help, as suggested by Marcia Eaton, because it might draw our attention to features of the works we would otherwise ignore. Above all else, we must approach art with an open mind. People who do this best are called "experts."

Expertise in the fine arts, as I suggested in the last chapter, is a function of exposure to various art forms, sensitivity, training, and openness to what is happening on the canvas, stage, or screen or in the music hall or text. The personal element enters into the judgments of the "experts," as it does with the rest of us, and at times, it tends to throw off the judgment and blinds them to something new and subtle. This is frequently the case with "new wave" art, as it was with Mahler's First Symphony and Stravinsky's "Firebird" when they were first performed. In such cases, we discover critics trying to view new art through old lenses. The fact that this does occur does not make the case for relativism, however. Usually, we reflect later and say that the critics were *wrong* in their assessment of what the artist was trying to do. And this judgment is a claim for which we are prepared to bring forward reasons. The fact that experts can make mistakes simply means that they, like us, are human. It does not denigrate the notion of expertise.

Because the factors that enter into the artistic transaction vary from individual to individual and because the art object is an object for a subject, it is impossible to eradicate the subjective factors present in the artistic transaction. But it is a mistake, as I have insisted above, to reduce the object to those subjective factors. The point has been made most persuasively by Vernon Lee in elaborating his distinction between listening to and merely hearing music, quoted above. Recall that he lists such elements as pitch, intervals, modulations, rhythms, and intensities—elements that make up values—as constitutive of "the meaning of music . . . the meaning not in the sense of a message different from whatever conveys it, but in the sense of an interest, an importance, residing in the music and inseparable from it" (Lee 1933, 33).

Discussion in art can progress toward consensus only if we continue to draw attention to the object and to increase our awareness of those stubborn subjective factors that tend to stand between us and the object and render it opaque. But in the end, it is the object that is found to be valuable or lacking in value.

Notes

1. Colin Martindale noted in a recent article that the question of the presence or absence of features in works of art and literature is an empirical, not a theoretical, question. Accordingly, he conducted a series of experiments with a variety of readers and listeners that led him to conclude that "there is something *in* a work of art that compels one to perceive it in one or another way. The reader does not create the text." In fact, his experiments also showed that experts tend to agree more than nonexperts, even though there is a remarkable level of agreement within the latter group as well (Martindale 1996, 359).

Although I would not want to reduce questions of value to the opinions of spectators, nonetheless, it is striking what one finds out when asking people what they see and hear. Opinions can be suggestive, if not conclusive. For a number of years, for example, I conducted tests somewhat similar to Martindale's in my own aesthetics classes. I played brief selections from classical music and then asked my students to choose from a list of regional properties the one that best described the mood of the piece (such words as *gay, melancholy,* or *frightening*). The incidence of agreement was always uniformly high in a group that, by its own admission, was not well versed in classical music. In fact, agreement was never below chance and was at times as high as 90 percent. My "experiments" were not as rigorous as Martindale's, but they, too, confirmed his conclusion that "there is something *in* a work of art or literature that determines the work's impact" (Martindale 1996, 359).

2. A most interesting example of "requiredness" as regards the creative process is provided by Françoise Gilot's account of a moment during Picasso's painting of her portrait. She tells us:

> Suddenly he remembered that Matisse had spoken of doing my portrait with green hair and he fell in with the suggestion. "Matisse isn't the only one who can paint you with green hair," he said. From that point the hair developed into a leaf form, and once he had done

that the portrait resolved itself into a symbolic floral pattern. . . . The face had remained quite realistic during these phases. . . . He studied it for a moment. "I have to bring in the face on the basis of another idea," he said. . . . Even though you have a fairly long oval face, what you need in order to show its light and expression, is to make it a wide oval. I'll compensate for the length by making it a cold color—blue. It will be like a little moon."

He painted a sheet of paper sky-blue and began to cut out oval shapes corresponding in varying degrees to the concept of my head. . . . Then he pinned them on to the canvas, one after another, moving each one a little bit to the left or right, up or down, as it suited him. None struck him as appropriate until he reached the last one. . . . He stuck it to the canvas, stood aside, and said, "Now it's your portrait." (Françoise Gilot and Carleton Lake, *Life with Picasso* [New York: McGraw-Hill, 1964], 117)

Chapter 6

Greatness in Literature

The texts I want to read from the deconstructive point of view are texts I love. . . . They are texts whose future, I think, will not be exhausted for a long time.
—Jacques Derrida

As noted in the third chapter, postmodern critics make a great deal out of the fact that people's notions of what the text says change over time. I would go even further than these critics do and note that what people interpret the text to say varies from time to time among different people within the same culture and that even the same person's interpretation can change from moment to moment. It does not follow from this, as I argued, that there are no texts, nor does it follow that the idea of greatness cannot be attached to some of them. I propose in this chapter to stand the rejection of the concept of the text on its head: I suggest that this variety of interpretations can be viewed as testimony to the text's singularity and its greatness as a work of art.

What the deconstructionists have referred to as the text's "undecidability" is precisely what the New Critics once called its "ineffaceable and ineradicable ambiguity," which they regarded as one of the chief marks of its excellence.[1] Unlike an essay or a philosophical treatise, which are discursive and whose language therefore demands univocal meanings, works of literature—as expressions of the human imagination—are fundamentally ambiguous. Mikhail Bahktin stressed repeatedly the distinctive nature of literature *as art* and touted the "dialogical" power of the novelist's imagination—namely, its capacity (in the case of Dostoyevsky, at least) to "project a plurality of independent and unmerged voices and consciousnesses, and the genuine polyphony of full-valued voices" (Bahktin 1973, 4). This "polyphony" results from the multiplicity of voices that can be heard in the novel as well as from the rich texture of the language itself. These "voices" constitute the novel's value as art.

The apparently limitless possibilities of the meanings of a literary text do not make the text itself disappear behind a shroud; rather, they define—initially, at any rate—one measure of the novel's greatness. As William Gass has noted in this regard, "From any given body of fictional text [if it is any good], nothing necessarily follows, and anything plausible may" (Gass 1977, 36).

A great work of literature, being a work of art, will exhibit a variety of perspectives, inherent and ineluctable ambiguities, that often hide the author from view and generate a host of plausible interpretations. Further, it will be exemplary in both form and matter—well written in the sense that its style is suitably adapted to its subject, deserving of imitation, and universal in its suggestion. As a work of art, it focuses on the particular, but the particular embodies the universal: the characters in a great novel are not us, but they are like us. They are unique, but we learn about ourselves and about others by coming into contact with them. Let us see how this happens in a particular case.

Hamlet lives in the pages of Shakespeare's play, in the performance on the stage, and in the minds of those who listen with their hearts to his agony of indecision—which is, at times, our own as well. He is a particular young man who is, for the moment, the embodiment of melancholia. We say that he is "melancholic," of course, not that he is "melancholia." But for the moment, he is both: he is the embodiment in a concrete particular of a universal, and we come to know the condition in its full presentational immediacy as we experience the play. Hamlet "symbolizes" melancholia in Goethe's sense of that term: Hamlet is "a true symbol [in which] the particular represents the universal, not as a dream or a shadow, but as living and instantaneous revelation of the unfathomable" (Goethe n.d., 266). Only the genius of the poetic imagination makes possible the embodiment of the universal in this particular person, who remains particular, even singular, despite carrying with him deep human significance; this is a sure sign of greatness.

Additionally, the great novel will be inherently interesting; it will have the power to attract and hold the attention of any sensitive reader who is willing to make the effort of imagination required of all art, to adopt what I have called "the aesthetic standpoint." That is to say, great literature is "great" precisely because it is an excellent work of art, an exemplary work of the human imagination. Literature must be measured as art, then, since this is where it succeeds or fails as great literature.

This point is central and requires amplification. "Literature," in the present context, means works of fiction, as contrasted with works of poetry and nonfiction. Poetry clearly is art, whereas nonfiction clearly is not, though it can also achieve "greatness." In nonfiction, content is central, since such works can be regarded as great simply because they are historically important—regardless of how badly written they happen to be. Historical importance is judged by the work's impact on the subsequent history of ideas—whether or not the work is also judged to be somehow "correct" or "right." Thus, Adam Smith's *Wealth of Nations* is judged to be a great book because of its impact on the history of economics, despite the fact that the labor theory of value is now regarded as "wrongheaded." As it happens, this particular book is also well written, and when this is the case, we can find the common thread between great works of nonfiction and great works of fiction: they both exemplify what human beings are capable of when they are most thoughtful and creative, when they have something to say and say it well.

Works of fiction, on the other hand, are also works of art—though they are a special case, as most aestheticians agree. It is their status as works of art that requires us to measure their greatness in terms of ambiguity, which is to say, their many possible meanings. This is what is essential in all good art. Critics generally acknowledge that a work of fiction suffers if it is didactic, if it seeks to make a point. This is because ambiguity is the *sine qua non* of the greatness of literature *qua* art. Thus, even exceptionally well written novels, such as *Things Fall Apart* or *Hard Times,* fail to achieve greatness because they speak with one voice instead of many, and that voice is the author's own. No matter how important the author's message is, if the novel simply becomes a platform, it cannot be considered great literature. In fiction that succeeds, the *novelist* remains in control, whereas in fiction that fails as art, the *person* has taken over. In the latter case, it is only too clear what the reader is to think in the end. This is why, for example, D.H. Lawrence is so much more the artist in *Women in Love* than he is in *Aaron's Rod*—because the novelist is in control in the former case whereas the man has taken over in the latter. So, too, in the case of the Dickens novel mentioned above, as well as in Chinua Achebe's novel—as I shall show in some detail later in this chapter.

The ineluctable ambiguity that emerges from the plethora of values at the center of every great work of art makes it great, and this is true of works of literature no less than it is of paintings, poems, and musical compositions.

⁓

We have it on good authority that all art aspires to the condition of music. In this regard, the musicologist Leonard Meyer has told us that greatness in music is a function of what he calls "information conveyed economically" (Meyer 1967, 37). Now since music is almost totally devoid of subject matter—with the possible exception of "programmatic" music—it is clear that "information" does not refer to what the music is about. Rather, as noted in the last chapter, Meyer is referring to that which is new and unexpected, that which is original and engages our imagination. Great music exhibits superb "syntactical organization" coupled with a great many "improbabilities" so that our response is one of surprise and delight (Meyer 1967, 36). The parallel between music and literature is not exact; nonetheless, it is informative. We reduce the novel to its subject matter at the risk of ignoring its status as a work of art. As art, it is full of meanings that often conflict with one another, some more apparent than others. Like the wrathful in Dante's *Inferno*, meanings appear and disappear in the river of blood and are hard to make out in the dim light of ambiguity. This ambiguity is not to be decried; it marks the strength of the work of art: it sets it apart as a work of the human imagination. Because of this ineluctable ambiguity, the novel does not have "a point"; it has many.

As a result, it yields multiple interpretations and invites repeated reading. In addition, a great work of literature is also well crafted, stylistically elegant, and rich in texture, vocabulary, and symbolism. Its language reveals a complex conceptual and imaginative framework, together with the high levels of emotional and ideational conflict alluded to above.

A novel is great, then, because it achieves an exceptionally high level of expression as a work of art. When we consider it as a work of art, we must consider it in its totality, as subject matter informed by the novelist into a new substantial whole. The sensitive reader, like the discerning spectator in the fine arts, must engage the work fully on its own terms. Reducing the novel to either form or matter by focusing exclusively on what it says while ignoring how it is said is to treat the novel as something other than itself.

To be sure, there are limits to the number of stylistic flaws that can be permitted if the work is to be considered great. Also, the level of objectionable subject matter can be high enough to offend even the most tolerant reader. In either case, it is impossible to engage the work fully, and the work is therefore flawed *as a work of art.* A poorly written novel does not reveal any of the novelist's meanings; on the other hand, if the subject matter is simply passed along to the reader without being informed by the novelist in the creative process, it will not engage the reader's imagination. In neither case is it art. If, further, the subject matter is such that it cannot *possibly* be engaged as a work of art, then the work is fundamentally flawed. This is a tough call, and the question can be settled only by a jury of trained, sensitive readers and must focus on evidence within the novel—bearing in mind how difficult it is to separate that which elicits a response from the response itself.

It is difficult to say, as a general rule, that morally unacceptable content (racism, for example) can *never* disable a work of art because of the many variables mentioned above. The issue must be raised case by case. One thinks of the flagrant sexism in the *Iliad* and in many of Shakespeare's plays, the anti-Semitism in many of Dostoyevsky's novels, and the misogyny in the plays of Euripides. But these works stand by virtue of the poetic hold they maintain on the reader's imagination.

In a word, questions of style and objections to subject matter are germane in criticism. But a novel can achieve greatness despite stylistic flaws or morally objectionable subject matter. To be sure, in an extreme case, a novel that depicts graphic violence, sexism, racism, or pornography or incorporates sensationalistic effects for their own sake will fail as a work of art. Indeed, it is not art at all; it is mere document. It also seems safe to say that novels that do not merely depict but actually foster or promote hatred or violence between or among peoples—regardless of how well they are written—cannot be viewed as great works of art because they are propaganda, not art.

~

It would appear that I have proposed a number of categories with which we can begin, at least, to determine what it is that makes literary works great. Barbara Herrnstein Smith would reject these categories, of course, as she has all standards, since they are in her view arbitrary. She insists, for example, that "all axiological arguments . . . enact a characteristic array of self-cancelling moves" (Smith 1988, 54). In a word, any attempt to posit standards of evaluation involves "an infinite regress" (Smith 1988, 63). If we ask how we know that the things I have suggested are necessary to determine greatness in literature, our attention is directed toward great works. Herein lies the regress—or at the very least, a vicious circle.

Indeed, this is the tactic I have adopted here, because I regard the works themselves as the final court of appeal. But it is precisely because it is the *final* court of appeal that the apparent circularity in devising criteria for evaluating greatness in literature is not vicious. The method suggested here resembles the hypothetico-deductive method of the natural scientist who observes regularity and then devises a rule or hypothesis that allows him or her to explain that regularity and make fruitful predictions on the basis of it.

When Charles Darwin, for example, formulated his theory of natural selection, he took some vaguely stated ideas from previous naturalists such as Lamarck and Malthus and wove them together into a highly original hypothesis to explain the origin of species. The phenomenon itself had been around since the beginning of animal life, and early thinkers such as Empedocles and Anaximander had devised primitive evolutionary theories to explain it, but these were brushed aside and ignored for two thousand years by Aristotle's heavy authority. In the years just prior to Darwin's formulation of the theory, such diverse thinkers as Goethe and Geoffroy had been struggling with a similar hypothesis, though they never quite got it right. Once Darwin pulled these threads together and formulated his hypothesis, its elegance and explanatory power lent it weight, and it gradually gained the status of a principle. No previous theory had explained the phenomena as simply or as elegantly.

The thing to note in this story is the process of discovery and formulation that precedes the testing of the hypothesis. The phenomena do not come out of thin air, nor are they a conjury on the part of an imaginative theorist. New species had been evolving for centuries. But it took an exceptional mind to discover the regularity that appeared through the mist of bias and misconception and formulate a hypothesis to explain that regularity. Once the hypothesis was formulated, it was then tested and confirmed by subsequent observation. Clearly, this is a circular process, as John Stuart

Mill has pointed out. The naturalist presupposes the regularity of nature in order to formulate a hypothesis to explain that regularity, which he or she then corroborates by reference back to nature. Despite its circularity, however, it works with remarkable success, and only the very stubborn can deny its explanatory power. In the end, the process is essentially pragmatic, but without it, we simply do not understand our world.

Similarly, we come to know what makes novels great by coming into contact with the novels and abstracting from them the values we recognize as distinctive in such works. As we read more, we gradually realize that the same values appear in other works and are absent in yet others. The former we call great; the latter we do not. In part, at least, it is because the latter lack the power to command our attention and affect us deeply. Great works, on the other hand, defy reduction to formulas or translation into other terms: we must meet them on their own ground. We know these works to be paradigmatic; they are well written, and they are significant—what they say speaks to all of us about what it means to be human. We do not pick these works at random, abstract properties from them whimsically, and then turn around and apply these properties to other works we then designate as "great." We recognize greatness when we see it because it "requires" our positive response. We then come to realize what, exactly, it is about those works that makes them great by a process that Charles Peirce called "abduction." The circularity in this reasoning is not vicious any more than is that of the natural scientist. Moreover, there is no regress either, because the process begins and ends with the works themselves.

~~~

Needless to say, the criteria I have suggested here are not meant as sharp weapons to allow us to slice up novels the way a cook cuts up whole carrots for a stew, putting some pieces in the pot and discarding others. But they will allow us to make legitimate discriminations among lesser and greater works. We need not abandon either the notion of the "text" or the contention that some works are great whereas others are not. To drive home the point, I shall contrast two novels in light of the criteria suggested above. These are two first novels, one written in recent times and another from an earlier era.

Chinua Achebe's *Things Fall Apart* has recently loomed large on the literary horizon and is certainly an important work. I would contend, however, that it is an important and well-written document, but it is not great literature for the reasons given above. It lacks the multiplicity of voices that are essential to works of art. Further, the author obtrudes upon the reader and makes it very clear where he stands; he does not let the novel speak for itself but uses it as a platform to make a point. What is central, from the perspective of criticism, is that by the end of the novel—which begins with great promise—Achebe the man has taken control, and Achebe the novelist has been rudely shouldered aside. Let us take a close look at just where this occurs.

Despite the fact that he is opposed by Okonkwo from the moment of his arrival, the missionary, Mr. Brown, is not a heartless man, and he does some good things in rescuing outcasts and abandoned infants from the Evil

Forest. For a time after the missionary arrives, Achebe manages to sustain considerable dramatic tension between him and the novel's main character. Indeed, Mr. Brown is portrayed as a kind man who tries to keep an open mind, while at the same time he is determined to impose his way of life on the natives. Okonkwo's son Nwoye is used most ingeniously as a pawn in a game the two men play, and when the boy converts to Christianity, the reader's sympathies are with both the son, who is miserable, and the father, who, despite himself, loves his son.

But when Brown is replaced by James Smith and the government joins forces with the Church, the tension disappears and the novel degenerates: Nwoye is forgotten; the good natives, who are clearly in the right, are set against the bad outsiders, who are clearly in the wrong. If this is not immediately obvious to us, Smith is joined by the diabolical district commissioner and his bullyboys, and the group becomes the embodiment of evil, less a poetic device than an abstract idea. Achebe the man is upset (and with good reason), but he lets his distress overpower his poetic imagination, and the novel tumbles from the higher levels of genuine dramatic tension and conflict, which are essential to great art. By the end of the novel, Achebe's rage has gotten the better of him, and the man has pinned the novelist to the mat. It was no contest. We have melodrama rather than drama: we are not allowed to form an opinion, because the author has already done it for us. And when the bullyboys "win out" and Okonkwo hangs himself, we share the author's rage and frustration and feel deep sadness. But that is precisely what Achebe wants us to feel: we are merely following doctor's orders. This is not great art; it is message.[2]

Achebe manages to create some uncertainties in the reader early in his novel by making his hero irascible and hard-hearted in his treatment of those who love him. He thus becomes an interesting and somewhat complex character, and the author takes the reader partway, at least, toward an understanding of Okonkwo, even, at times, generating sympathy for a man with deep-seated insecurities. For a time, as noted above, Achebe's inspiration rises to the level of art with these subtle complexities of character—especially when they come into conflict with the basically likable Mr. Brown. But Achebe is unable to sustain the dramatic tensions, as we saw, and must rely upon the reader's ordinary sensibilities to carry the novel through to its completion. The novel fails as art precisely as it succeeds as melodrama. In Mikhail Bahktin's terminology, Achebe's novel remains on the First Stylistic Level of the early European novels of chivalry parodied by Cervantes, evoking pathos and sentimentality rather than true sentiment and a distinctly aesthetic response (Bahktin 1981, 396 ff.).

Contrast this first novel by a young author with another first novel that shows signs of longer gestation and a higher artistic inspiration. We know that Jane Austen's *Pride and Prejudice* is a reworking of her earliest novel, *First Impressions,* and the alteration in the title reflects the maturing of her poetic vision.

Austen exhibits the control of the true artist throughout her novel until the very end, when she seems determined, like so many novelists of that period, to tie up all the loose ends. For the most part, the poet remains in control, and Austen creates marvelous dramatic uncertainties that circle around the book's very title. Who, exactly, personifies "pride," and who personifies "prejudice"? At first blush, it would appear that it is Mr. Darcy and Elizabeth Bennett, respectively. But Austen will not leave it at that. She suggests to the reader on numerous occasions that her two main characters are Janus-faced, and whereas Elizabeth "personifies" prejudice, she also exhibits pride, to a fault. She is proud of her perspicacity and her (seemingly) unfailing character studies. Darcy, too, exhibits deep-seated prejudices—against the Bennett family, for example. This complexity is central to the novel and is one of the ways Austen refracts the authorial perspective that is so noticeable in Achebe's novel. The reader is shown Elizabeth Bennett's weaknesses just as clearly as her strengths. Thus does Austen's novel easily reach Bahktin's Second Stylistic Level by exhibiting "double-voicedness" and "gay deception" (Bahktin 1981, 401). Austen further augments these stylistic devices by means of her brilliant comic sense and her ability to parody—not only in the cases of Mr. Collins and Lady Catherine DeBurgh but also in the case of Elizabeth and Mr. Darcy, who are both, in a profound sense, "comical."

Achebe's novel, in contrast, lacks any sense of the comical, and the author exhibits no love of parody (which is not to be confused with sarcasm and character assassination). Thus, he fails to keep the distance that is essential not only to the humorist and satirist but also to the artist. This is what keeps his novel from reaching the level of artistic greatness.

The control of the poet, as artist, must be subtle, but it

must also be certain. With Austen, it is (up to the end), whereas with Achebe, the poet soon loses control of the novel. Achebe the man is angry, and he wants his readers to share his anger. Jane Austen, on the other hand, has something important to say about the human spirit, and she respects her readers enough to let them engage the work in their own distinctive ways.

With these examples in mind, we can return to the question of the "greatness" of literary works, of which *Pride and Prejudice* is a case in point.

⁓

The view that there are texts and that some are really (in fact) "great" whereas others are not implies, of course, that some readers are better able than others to make these determinations. To the alert ears of critics like Barbara Herrnstein Smith, it thus begins to sound as if the "establishment axiologists" are taking over. As she remarks, apparently aghast, this would mean that "in matters of taste most of the people in the world are substandard or deviant" (Smith 1988, 37).

But surely, in matters of taste, most people *are* "substandard or deviant." In fact, "most of the people in the world" cannot read! Further, of those who are able to read, many do not bother (for whatever reason), and many who do read do so indiscriminately. The fact is that some people are better readers than others. I am better than some, but there are many others who are better than I. The most careful reader of novels I ever came into contact with was Eliseo Vivas.

The basis of Smith's objection is a confusion between

the respect we owe to others as moral agents and the legitimate distinctions we make among persons of differing abilities. All persons are morally equal, but they are not equally talented. Reading is a difficult and demanding activity when done properly, and not everyone is willing or able to make the effort.

It will be objected, however, that "we" are "privileging ourselves" in the above account of method. This would be so if we could identify those who make up this group, who the "we" happens to be, and if "we" happen always to be members of this group. Unfortunately, or fortunately, none of this happens to be so. The group is seldom the same from moment to moment, and "we" are at times excluded or marginalized by virtue of the peculiar nature of our likes and dislikes or because we cannot get past our prejudices. The process of determining which works are great and which are not is dynamic, and the methods employed are dialectical. They presuppose broad acquaintance with a variety of literary works, sensitivity to the nuances of the text and, above all else, an open mind. "We" do not always exhibit these qualities. No one does all the time.

The issue here is not one of "privileging the self"; it is an issue of "privileging expertise," which "we" may or may not happen to possess. Often the Other is not the one requiring "pathologising" (Smith's term); the self can also be Other. Status is not the issue, however; sensitivity to the written word is the issue.

Surely, it is reasonable to insist that some readers are better able than others, on the whole, to discern those peculiar features of literary works that make them truly worthwhile. Such people tend to evidence greater awareness of what is taking place in the novel itself than the rest of us, and they know where and how to look and listen: they are familiar with the language the artist uses to communicate, and their experience of literature is broad and wide-ranging. Such admissions fall short of allowing that there are experts who are *invariably* correct and therefore worthy of holding the keys to the treasures of great art. As acknowledged in the last chapter, the "experts" do not always agree. This is not, however, as significant as some would make it out to be. "Expertise" does not imply "infallibility." When our cars fail to perform properly, after all, we continue to take them to a mechanic—despite the fact that mechanics are sometimes mistaken.

Thus, it would seem to follow that, whereas every opinion deserves to be heard, the opinions of the experts are more likely to converge toward agreement and to be, if not "correct," then at least plausible. The test, of course, has nothing to do with credentials (though we would hope that our critics are well read). The test is found in the abilities of some people to reveal features of works of art to others who previously missed them. Works are not "great" because an expert says they are. They are great because they embody extraordinary values, and the experts are simply those who are, on balance, more likely to recognize greatness when it stares them in the face or peeks out from behind a bush. These people do not "conspire," as Smith and others have implied; they struggle to communicate with us and with one another—and to reach some sort of consensus.

It does not follow from anything I have said that everyone will agree, in fact, about what is or is not "great" art or what should or should not be included in the "canon of high culture." Further, it does not follow from what I have said that the canon as it stands is "correct" or that works of art that have been excluded from that canon are, *ipso facto*, inferior to those that are included. In fact, I have not said much about the canon at all and have restricted my attention to literary works—to the question of whether or not there are novels that can be called "great." Perhaps we would be well advised to routinely rethink the entire question of what should or should not compose the canon. But if we do, we must somehow penetrate the thick mist of our particular "economies" and make our determinations on the basis of what is present in or missing from the works themselves.

To allude once again to the "parable" quoted in my introduction, it is always possible that Sancho's wine-tasting relatives were conspiring to fool the assembled crowd. But to decide this, we should examine the empty wine cask and see whether or not it contains a key on a leather thong.

Notes

1. The term *undecidability* is from Ross Murfin's discussion of deconstructive criticism in *Hamlet,* edited by Susanne L. Wofford (1994, 289). Murfin insists that the "undecidability" of the deconstructionists is not the same thing as the ambiguity insisted upon by the New Critics. I suspect Murfin's bias against New Criticism is showing here, because the two look very similar. Murfin is surely wrong, furthermore, when he says that, for the New Critics, the ambiguity of literary texts can be eliminated ("the formalist [New] critic ultimately makes sense of ambiguity"). This is certainly not the case with Eliseo Vivas, who was once called "the aesthetician of the group [of New Critics]," for whom the novel's "ineffaceable and ineradicable" ambiguity is its distinctive

feature. See, for example, "Dostoyevsky, 'Poet' in Spite of Himself," in *Vivas as Critic,* edited by Hugh Curtler (New York: Whitston Press, 1982), 208.

2. Achebe would not agree with this criticism, of course. He claims that "poetry surely can only be on the side of man's deliverance and not his enslavement." My point is that poets cannot take sides and remain poets. I have responded at length to Achebe in my essay "Achebe on Conrad: Racism and Greatness in *Heart of Darkness.*" *Conradiana* 29, no. 1 (1997).

Chapter 7

Values and the Great Conversation

Education is the bringing up of one not to live alone,
but amongst others.

—Richard Mulcaster (1581)

Postmodernism has given birth to cultural pluralism, the view that an appreciation of differing cultures will enhance our perspective and enable us to better appreciate our world. As a movement, it is inexorable and will only get stronger, which is a mixed blessing. To the extent that it makes us aware of different ways of encountering our world and awakens us to our own cultural bias, smugness, and puffery, the movement is long overdue. But the adherents of one branch of the movement, which might be called "militant multiculturalism," stress human differences out of total disregard for human commonality.

Militant multiculturalism is characterized by repressive tolerance: while preaching openness to other points of

145

view, the movement is deaf to those who would raise legitimate questions of worth and attempt to discriminate among the hodgepodge of cultural convictions. All such convictions, it is said, are ideological, and predictably, value judgments are ruled out of court. Militant multiculturalism is thoroughly postmodern in its movement toward relativism, exclusivity, and reductionism. In this form, cultural pluralism bears close scrutiny as it seeks to elbow its way to a place at the table of higher education, which is already overcrowded and inadequate to feed the hungry.

Because of its inexorability, it would be fatuous to question whether or not we should continue to move in the direction of cultural pluralism. So I shall not do so. Further, I would be quick to admit that there are distinct advantages to Western high culture in being open to other ways of regarding the world; and if the canon of high culture cannot withstand the current critique by adherents of pluralism, that in itself may be a sign of inherent weakness in the dominant culture. My purpose in this chapter, however, is not to engage the larger issue but, rather, to examine some of the dangers that lurk at the center of multiculturalism, especially with respect to what I have called "inverted consciousness" and the rediscovery of values.

Contrasted with America in this century, no nation on earth has ever placed before its people a richer cornucopia of goods with fewer restrictions on choice. But although Americans are justifiably proud of the freedom this gives them, freedom is not reducible to the many options this abundance makes possible. A person is not free, for example, simply because she sees before her a bewildering variety of goods and has money in her pocket; that person is truly free only if she can order that variety and make it less bewildering.

In one sense, freedom increases as the number of choices increase. But freedom also involves *informed* choice, and information together with heightened powers of discrimination actually *reduce* the number of choices to the few that are worthy of serious consideration. This sort of freedom is called "positive freedom" or "autonomy" to the extent that such choices are our own and not foisted upon us by someone else. It contrasts with "negative freedom," or freedom viewed simply as the number of choices available at any moment.

Unlike negative freedom, positive freedom is not a function of birth or fortunate circumstances. Autonomy is true "self-empowerment," and it must be achieved through effort, increased understanding, and the development of intellect—abilities traditionally fostered by the liberal arts. It might be good to remind ourselves what these arts are and what it is they do.

Aristotle coined the term *art* to connote "knowledge of universals" applied by practical reason to concrete problems of the *polis,* or civic community. Western tradition has followed this usage, but it has recently come under attack by militant multiculturalists as being unduly narrow and restricted. This charge will not stand.

The trivium of grammar, logic, and rhetoric and the quadrivium of arithmetic, geometry, astronomy, and music constituted the original seven liberal arts formulated during the Middle Ages. These seven arts have proliferated until now the liberal arts include all those disciplines within the humanities, social sciences, and natural sciences that, through increased understanding, free the human mind from enslavement to inclination, habit, and passion. This is the current interpretation of what Aristotle meant when he spoke of "knowledge of universals" applied by practical reason. It is hardly a narrow focus, and it hardly favors one gender or ethnic group, because it is centered around a common human need.

I would note in passing that the liberal arts are not "techniques." They do not focus on "know-how," as does so much of what is currently taught in our colleges and universities. The liberal arts liberate the human mind by enabling it to make disciplined, informed choices. Such choices are made every day when we try to decide which politician to believe this year, how we ought to vote on the upcoming referendum, whether or not we ought to boycott a local bank that exploits women, or even such a frivolous issue as what car to buy. To the extent that a person is autonomous, he or she will be able to resist demagoguery, hucksterism, coercion, and intimidation; recognize exaggeration and prevarication; distinguish between the true and the false, and between an opinion that is supported by evidence and argument and one that merely feels comfortable. These are essential abilities, and once again, they are hardly narrow or culture-specific.

In this regard, the opinion recently expressed by Halford Fairchild that learning myths about their African ancestors "empowers black people" reflects serious confusion about the nature of autonomy and "power" (Fairchild 1995, 162). One cannot achieve autonomy, or power over self, through ignorance in any of its various guises, since ignorance makes each of us susceptible to suggestion and persuasion by someone else. The only effective way to achieve *self-determination* is through knowledge. If, for example, I know that Senator Jones is a bigot and in the pocket of special-interest groups, then I will be less easily swayed by his campaign rhetoric, though, of course, he may speak the truth in spite of himself. If I am in the dark about the man, and especially if I cannot follow his arguments or recognize unsound reasoning, then I can easily be swept up by what he says and his manner of saying it. If what he says sounds good, I am likely to believe it. If I am to make an informed judgment, I must be able to distinguish between what "sounds good" and what rings true. If we abandon the ideal of objective truth and the possibility of separating knowing from supposing, we have nothing to fall back on but what we like to hear. That is not an adequate base upon which to build genuine empowerment, since others will quickly recognize our ignorance and maintain a hold over us by telling us what they know we want to hear.

Autonomy means the power of the self over itself, subject to no determination from outside agencies. This is not possible if we allow myths to parade as the truth, no matter how pleasant the myths and how unpleasant the truth. Autonomy must remain the goal of education, and open discussion, debate, and genuine dialogue about what is and is not true—in accordance with accepted methodologies and public criteria of evidence—are the only ways we can ever hope to reach that goal. In our frenzy for diversity, we must remind ourselves, in the words of Mary Lefkowitz, that "the notion of diversity does not extend to truth" (Lefkowitz 1996, 162).

The liberal arts presuppose a common human nature, because education has as its goal the realization of the specifically human in all persons. The moral perspective that arises from such a focus on equality is in direct conflict with a militant doctrine of multiculturalism that would "privilege difference" to the exclusion of the commonality that subtends all differences. In terms of higher education, this type of multiculturalism tends to fractionalize a purpose that becomes weaker as it loses focus. The academy cannot be all things to all people, and if it does not focus on its special purpose—that which makes it unique among social institutions—it will do nothing well. The purpose of higher education is not to hammer preconceptions about social justice into the captive minds of students but to put these people in possession of their *own* minds. If we are serious about achieving social justice, we will acknowledge that educating free men and women is the best way to reach that goal.

The purpose of education centers around a need that is common to all people at all times, because all people everywhere need to be free. One of the dangers of multiculturalism is that, in concentrating on human particularity, our common human nature, which ought always to remain at the center of any discussion of the purpose of liberal education, is ignored or denied altogether. As Giambattista Vico noted long ago, despite the fact that we speak different languages, we all use language, and one of the goals of liberal education has always been to enable each of us to use it effectively.

For the Greeks, of course, this goal required involvement in the *polis* or, as Aristotle would have it, the exercise of civic virtue. What is of chief interest to us today about this somewhat archaic notion—which was, of course, restricted to propertied males—is that education was regarded as the vehicle by which young people became law-abiding members of a human group. The *polis* was at once a political, intellectual, and moral community in which participation was essential if people were to become fully human. This required that those who would practice civic virtue develop the skills that might enable them to become full-fledged members of their community—skills of speaking, writing, listening, reasoning, and figuring. From our contemporary perspective, of course, "people" includes all persons and not only propertied males; the community of which we are a part is no longer the *polis,* it is the world; and citizenship means membership in the world community.

The controlling idea of Aristotle's political philosophy was the notion that healthy states differ from unhealthy states because the former concern themselves with the *common* good whereas the latter splinter into multiple concerns about particular goods—usually centered around the short-term self-interest of particular citizens. Rousseau later called groups preoccupied with such particular goods "cabals and factions" and warned that they obtrude between citizens and "The General Will." This is not to say that we ought not to be motivated by self-interest: that would be absurd. What Aristotle and Rousseau both meant was that our notion of self-interest must encompass the interest of others. Civic virtue redirects attention outward toward what is best for all on the grounds that what benefits all of us benefits each of us. The practice of this sort of virtue requires the development of those skills of intellect and imagination that make it possible for us to envision consequences, sympathize with victims of injustice, and develop reasonable plans of action as members of a group, without which we are less than human. Above all else, it implies respect for the rule of law, which, under the best of circumstances, should be self-imposed. This is where citizenship and autonomy come together and why citizenship, properly understood, has always been at the center of any discussion of the purpose of liberal education. A liberal education fosters those skills that make involvement in the community possible and productive for autonomous citizens who are able to act intelligently in promoting the common good, which they recognize as their own good.

As I have noted, however, citizenship today means world citizenship and not merely membership in small communities of like-minded people. World citizenship maintains at its center the notion of autonomous agents interacting with other members of their community, whom they regard as their political equals with equal rights. The difference is that the community has now become all-inclusive, though the idea of political equality remains central. As Lisa Newton has said in another connection entirely, "If citizenship is not a possibility, political equality is unintelligible." If, then, citizenship is undermined, "none of us is . . . a citizen, a bearer of rights—we are all petitioners for favors" (Newton 1992, 72). The term *citizenship* was coined during the Enlightenment, and it retains its eighteenth-century commitment to the development of reason and respect for truth. These are peculiarly "modern" concepts, of course, but in our postmodern frenzy, we reject them at our peril.

Citizenship requires an ability to think critically and engage with others in dialogue in order to formulate reasoned judgments to which we submit willingly. If we cannot function in this world as citizens, we are indeed reduced to the status of "petitioners for favors." In such a world, there is no difference between reasoned judgment and personal opinion, communication has broken down, and confrontation has replaced dialogue as a means to adjudicate differences. Might, in such a world, does, in fact, make right.

For the individualist who is about to enter the twenty-first century, however, citizenship has little meaning. For those whose consciousness has turned in on itself and, as Ortega would have it, become "hermetically sealed," *community* is simply a nine-letter word. Such people are "from birth deficient in the faculty of giving attention to what is outside themselves," and for them, there is no community (Ortega 1960, 67).

As noted in the first chapter, however, citizenship is above all else the will to live in common. And world citizenship means membership in the community of all human beings. Individual*ism* takes us in the direction of militant multiculturalism, which "privileges difference," fosters exclusion, and takes us deeper into ourselves and further from one another. In this world, the "other" exists merely as a curiosity, nuisance, or source of pleasure or pain. From the perspective of education, young people must achieve individual*ity*—that is, they must mature; survive adolescence, during which self-absorption is appropriate; and willfully become members of the world community, without losing their uniqueness.

"Membership" is a complex concept, however, and goes beyond merely signing on the dotted line. It does not mean losing oneself in the whole, but it does involve a willing acceptance of the good of the whole as one's own good. As Joseph Tussman has noted with regard to membership in political communities, "To be a member of the body politic is thus to be a voluntary party to a basic agreement or system of agreements which involves the subordination of private to public interest and of private to public decision . . ." (Tussman 1970, 31).

The critical terms in Tussman's statement are *voluntary* and *subordination.* In order to be an effective member of any community, a person must achieve autonomy and be willing to subordinate short-term self-interest to the good of all members of the community. That is, a person must knowingly and willingly subordinate his or her will to the will of the group. How is this possible?

⌒

The most appropriate educational vehicle to bring us out of ourselves and into the world is the works of the greatest human minds that have ever lived. We must join what Robert Hutchins once called "the Great Conversation." I am not merely defending the current "canon" of the Western world, though, surely, this is where we must begin in thinking about what is worth teaching and learning. We must cull the treasures of all world civilizations to place before the young the most extraordinary works of their kind that have thus far been created. These works will require that they think deeply about serious human problems. Because these works are great, furthermore, readers will learn what is exemplary and what is worthy of imitation. But our criteria of selection must remain intellectual and aesthetic and not ideological. The issue is not which works I happen to agree with, or which authors happen to agree with me, but which are most disturbing and most worthy of serious attention. Though the word is anathema to the postmodern ear, we must not hesitate to discriminate: we cannot avoid value judgments. A few works are worthy of close attention and serious thought, but most are not. Only a few works can be considered "great."

As I have noted throughout this book, however, it has been charged that determinations of "greatness" cannot be made on intellectual or aesthetic grounds, that values reduce inevitably to ideology. Barbara Herrnstein Smith, recall, makes the claim that selection of "representative" works is driven by "culturally specific conditions" (Smith 1988, 52). As a result, "it is no surprise that 'essentially aesthetic experiences' always conform to those typical of the Western or Western-educated consumer of high culture and that 'essentially aesthetic value' always turns out to be located in the old familiar places and masterpieces" (Smith 1988, 36).

There are a number of things wrong with this claim. To begin with, it is quite simply false. Even a moment's reflection on the holdings of major galleries and museums in the West reveals a bewildering variety of artifacts from every possible culture from the beginning of time. Symphony orchestras are frequently conducted by non-Western people, and a great many chairs in those orchestras are occupied by women and minorities. Furthermore, even the most conservative of the preservers of high culture, such as Harold Bloom, include in their lists of "great books" works by a host of non-Western writers.

At this point, it might be wise to pause and reflect on a question that is seldom raised: just what *is* the "canon" of Western high culture that has been so severely criticized of late? I suggest that it is largely a piece of fiction, a straw man constructed for target practice. It suggests a monolithic body of knowledge that fosters a particular point of view. *There is no such thing.* Anyone familiar with these works will attest that a glance through even the narrowest of lists of great works of literature and philosophy will reveal no two thinkers who agree about much of anything. It is simply impossible to claim with any seriousness that the canon fosters a particular point of view. In fact, it is a polyglot of opinions on every possible issue that humans have ever thought about seriously. This variety of opinions both disarms the multiculturalist criticism and makes it essential reading on the part of any person who seeks to gain possession of his or her own mind. There is no single perspective being fostered in the canon. To insist that there is reveals an appalling ignorance of the works in question.

Attacks on the canon are off the mark and at times outrageous. Arguments often reduce to the level of *ad hominem* and propose rejection of great works of art and literature simply because they were produced by white, European males. This is as weak as the proposal to include works simply because they were *not* written by white, European males. There is every reason to insist upon public criteria for determining the worthiness of serious works of art and literature. Judgments must focus on the value of the works selected, whether or not they are worthy of serious consideration and whether or not they will engender autonomy.

The suggestion by critics that Western thinkers have been conditioned to prefer Western works—a sort of aesthetic brainwashing, if you will—cannot stand up to criticism. Any sophisticated reader who has been brought up on Western literature can pick up a novel by Kawabata, R.K. Narayan, or Jorge Luis Borges and recognize a work of genius. One need not change cultural spectacles when leaving a gallery filled with paintings by French impressionists to enter one filled with works by Japanese Zen painters. One need not unlearn old ways of seeing when sitting down to watch a film by Kurosawa, and reading the Upanishads is no more taxing for Western readers than reading Nietzsche's *Joyful Wisdom*. As I mentioned in my critique of Marcia Eaton's aesthetics in the fourth chapter, critics are right to stress the importance of tradition in learning the language of a particular artist or school. They are wrong to make this tradition the determining factor.

Works of genius have a commanding presence. Ortega was surely correct when he noted that "talking of genius is not an expression of praise; it is an experiential finding, a phenomenon of religious experience" (Ortega 1961, 72). If the Great Conversation is to include works by non-Western people, as it should, then those works must be selected because they merit serious attention and not because they "represent" other cultures. This is tokenism, literary affirmative action, taken to its worst, most warped extreme.

⌒

Barbara Herrnstein Smith is correct to point out a danger and a temptation, however. It is easy to become protective and even a bit smug about the works we prize. But she is wrong to insist that judgments of greatness are "always" reducible to cultural bias. It is quite possible that many, indeed most, of the greatest works of the human mind have been produced by Western culture. But we must beware the temptation to regard Western culture as in any sense "privileged." The fact that lists of "great" works include so many works by Western thinkers and artists may simply be the result of the sheer weight of numbers. Consider how many thousands of works by Western writers are *not* considered "great." At the same time, we must keep in mind that Western culture is one among many possible ways of seeing the world. Having said this, one must nonetheless begin in the search for what is truly worth serious attention with those works that have, with good reason, withstood the test of time. In this regard, George Steiner reminds us that "ninety nine percent of humanity . . . contributes nothing to the sum of insight, of beauty, or moral trial in our civil condition. It is a Socrates, a Mozart, a Gauss, or a Galileo who, in some degree, compensate for man. It is they who, on fragile occasion redeem the cruel, imbecile mass which we dignify with the name of history" (Steiner 1996, 275). Cut off from people such as these by postmodern zealots who, burdened by guilt and anxious to right past wrongs, deny difference and ignore greatness, we are diminished and wallow in a quagmire of mediocrity. We can deconstruct what great thinkers have said and show that they have feet of clay, but this does not diminish the sweep of their mind or the scope of their sensibilities.

The claim that the canon of high culture is simply the product of a particular power structure that seeks to maintain hegemony is palpably absurd. The canon bears the marks of genius. As such, the canon provides us with numerous paradigms of human wisdom and reveals us to ourselves in all our frailty and imperfection. That canon, after all, has taken us to the point where we now question its very foundations, and this is a healthy sign, indeed. This does not imply that the canon is closed. Rather, the discussion about what should make up the Great Conversation should remain an open question. If works need to be added, they should be, but the only relevant considerations in this regard are that these works should exhibit "mastery indicated by such virtues as scope, perspicacity, subtlety, power to illuminate, alertness to the antithesis, and command over intrinsic requirements of form" (Alvis 1933, 30). If specific works selected to be read fall short of the measure, they should be replaced by other works that do not. And if these works can reflect a variety of cultural outlooks, so much the better. What is critical in these determinations is not that the works we read reflect difference; what is critical is that they be exemplary, that new works rank as high on the scale of human achievement as the old. If the books we read are to prove liberating, they must take us outside of ourselves. They must embody exceptional values. The worst possible reason for selecting texts, from a pedagogical standpoint, is that the instructor agrees with the author. That is why great literature, as that notion was discussed in the last chapter, should be preferred: it is impossible to find the author's voice in the rich mixture that characterizes great literature. There is no better way for a student to find his or her own voice than to encounter many voices speaking eloquently.

To some readers, of course, my concern for resurrecting the concept of citizenship and refocusing attention on civic virtue will seem anachronistic. But to others, the demise of dialogue as a way of finding reasonable solutions to pressing human problems simply emphasizes the depth of our current need to recall the purpose of liberal education.

Unfortunately, as has been noted, multiculturalism does not concern itself with building a sense of community across cultural boundaries. Rather, it separates human cultures and subcultures by emphasizing their distinct vocabularies and particular worldviews. In fact, multiculturalism does regard each individual, culture, or subculture as a "petitioner for favors," a view that leads invariably toward confrontation and conflict. Such a view is distorted and partial; it ignores the common element among all human groups and the capacity of human beings to enter into dialogue with, and to understand, other human beings in spite of their differences. Referring to multiculturalism as "corporate pluralism," Anne Wortham has noted in this regard,

> Most of all, corporate pluralism denies the proposition that persons from different backgrounds can be united by ideas and values that transcend the interests, beliefs, and norms of particular groups and subcultures. Instead of promoting intergroup relations based on such universal criteria as rationality, personal autonomy, and individual rights, corporate pluralism affirms cultural particularism—the doctrine that persons belonging to different cultural groups should be treated differently.
>
> The multicultural education movement's efforts to impose "cultural diversity" on college and grade school curricula [are] fueled by just this particularism. (Wortham 1992, 37)

Seen in this light, multiculturalism is in direct opposition to the ideal of world citizenship that is defended here. But there seems little doubt that world citizenship is an idea whose realization has become a pressing need.

There are few, if any, purely local problems anymore. The issues that face humankind and demand thoughtful, effective remedies are global: overpopulation, famine, destruction of the environment, violence among and within cities, genocide, terrorism, and diseases that cause unnecessary human suffering. The ideological quarrels between the various special-interest groups within the academy, to the extent that they arise from a genuine concern for social justice, are worthy of serious attention and consideration. But these quarrels must take a back seat to those issues that relate directly to the survival of the species and the preservation of the planet. More to the point, they must take a back seat to the basic issue of how best to enable young people to come to grips with these problems in their own way. Perhaps we can deal with both the larger and the smaller issues at the same time; but ideological agendas have a way of intruding, and if we allow that to happen, our central purpose will almost certainly get lost in the frenzy to make converts.

The central concern of education—and it should be a concern of all who are disturbed by our current cultural crisis—is with autonomy and with the decreasing ability of our educational institutions to put young men and women in possession of their own minds. The way to do that is to invite them to become participants in the Great Conversation. This can happen only if we admit the legitimacy of values and the corollary that some contributions to that conversation are truly "great."

Postscript

In Defense of Values

Modern man is progressively losing his understanding of values and his sense of proportions. This failure to understand essential realities is extremely serious. It leads us infallibly to the violation of the fundamental laws of human equilibrium.

—Igor Stravinsky

So many postmodern thinkers echo the complaints of the youthful Nietzsche in his attacks on "the despotic logician" Socrates, the "theoretical optimist" given to the "delusion of limitless progress." In *The Birth of Tragedy,* Nietzsche cries out against the

> cheerfulness of the *theoretical man* ... [which] seeks to dissolve myth, substitutes for a metaphysical comfort an earthly consonance, in fact, a *deus ex machina* of its own, the god of machines and crucibles, that is, the powers of the spirits of nature recognized and employed in the service of a higher egoism; [which] believes that it can correct the world by knowledge, guide life by science, and actually confine the

individual within a limited sphere of solvable problems, from which he can cheerfully say to life, "I desire you; you are worth knowing." (*Birth of Tragedy* [*BT*], 109)

The complaints of Nietzsche's postmodern disciples, from Derrida to the meanest multiculturalist, reflect a similar revulsion over the barrenness of an exhausted culture, which they, too, blame on scientism. To be sure, as I admitted in the first chapter, there are solid grounds for this revulsion.

At the same time, we must beware the temptation to reject out of hand everything that stinks of modernism and the Enlightenment. We must resist the postmodern urge to reject and reduce in the conviction that everything Western humans thought prior to 1930 leads inevitably to the Holocaust and its aftermath and that every exemplary work of art and literature diminishes the human soul. In particular, we must maintain a firm hold on our intellectual center and, while acknowledging the need for greater compassion and heightened imaginative power, also acknowledge our need for reasonable solutions to complex issues.

Indeed, the rejection of reason and "techno-science" as it is voiced by such thinkers as Jean-François Lyotard seems at times little more than resentment born of a sense of betrayal: "it is no longer possible to call development progress" (Lyotard 1992, 78). Instead, modernism has given us Auschwitz. Therefore, we will blame reason and science as the vehicles that have brought us to this crisis. Reason has yielded technology, which has produced nuclear weapons, mindless diversions, and choking pollution in our cities while enslaving the human spirit. Therefore, we reject reason. This is odd logic. Reason becomes hypostatized and is somehow guilty of having made false promises. The fault may not lie with our tools or methods, however, but with the manner in which we adapted them and the tasks we demanded they perform. That is to say, the problem may lie not with our methods but with ourselves.

At times, one wonders whether thinkers such as Lyotard read Dostoyevsky, Freud, or Jung, whether they know anything about human depravity. Science is not at fault; foolish men and women (mostly men) who have expected the impossible of methods that were designed primarily to solve problems are at fault. We cannot blame science because we have made of it an idol. Lyotard was correct when he said that "scientific or technical discovery was never subordinate to demands arising from human needs. It was always driven by a dynamic independent of the things people might judge desirable, profitable, or comfortable" (Lyotard 1992, 83). But instead of focusing attention on the "dynamic," he chooses to reject the entire techno-scientific edifice. This is reactionary. We face serious problems, and the rejection of science and technology will lead us back to barbarism, not to nirvana. What is required is a lesson in how to control our methods and make them serve our needs. Thus, although one can sympathize with the postmodern attack on scientific myopia, one must urge caution in the face of hysteria. There are additional problems with postmodernism, however.

The major concern in this book has been the postmodern contribution to our present-day "hatred of values." I have argued that the postmodern rejection of values simply compounds a cultural attitude that has been dominant since the birth of the social sciences at the end of the last century. This attitude stems from a tendency to confuse values with evaluation, which, in turn, arises from the reduction of the world to the world-for-me, the fundamental inversion of human consciousness away from the world and toward the self who experiences that world. I shall elaborate briefly in bringing this discussion to a close.

Except, perhaps, during moments of ecstasy, human consciousness is intentional in that it always has an object. When that object becomes the human subject itself, there follows a reduction of all experience to personal experience and a diminished field of consciousness to the vanishing point of me-here-now. For example, instead of concentrating attention on what it is about the music that gives me joy, or what it is about the novel that makes it delightful, I focus attention on my own experience of the music or the novel, my own joy and my own delight. Instead of entering a relationship with another because I care about his or her happiness, my only concern is how that person makes me feel. On a larger scale, instead of worrying about water downstream, I make sure my factory operates efficiently and at a profit. Events, ideas, and values become personalized. In the process, I lose respect for the Other and concern for the common world we share: he, she, or it no longer matters; what matters is *my experience* of the Other and *my experience* of the world. The subject becomes the object of its own consciousness. This is "inverted consciousness," wherein the ego becomes, as Ortega noted with great foresight, "hermetically sealed."

In the end, the spirit of postmodernism is a spirit of rejection, and this is an inadequate basis on which to build new systems of learning. We must admit the limits of modernism while at the same time we salvage what is best and most promising—including the methods of the exact sciences and the analytical tools forged by philosophers since the time of Descartes. We must reject the tendency in postmodern thought to embrace relativism by reducing values to valuation, by denying the notion of greatness, and by paying excessive attention to personal perspectives.

As admitted in the second chapter, postmodernists are surely correct in saying that language can ensnare us and can be used by the unscrupulous to gain and maintain power. And they are also correct to say that we all bring with us our several "economies" when we judge behavior, read books, or attend concerts and galleries. But they are wrong to ignore the fact that education can enlighten and loosen the snares of language and to assume that our value judgments do not refer beyond ourselves to objects that are truly delightful or hideous. The insights of postmodern thinking must be acknowledged, but they must be balanced by a concern for its tendency toward reductionism, exclusivity, and obscurantism. One must also caution against its tendency to embrace half-truths and to exaggerate claims, despite their grounding in genuine insights.

The world is real, and values are features or aspects of that world that "require" our approval. Our experience of that world is created in the interplay between the subjective "economies" we bring with us and the stubborn aspects of objects not of our making. Whether or not the theoretical

debate is settled, the "fundamental laws of human equilibrium" of which Stravinsky speaks in the opening passage of
this chapter require that human beings once again turn their
attention away from themselves and cultivate a readiness to
enjoy and a determination to engage that can begin only
with a look at those aspects of the world that are not of our
own making. We must follow the Sufis and "return to the
World." That return begins with a rediscovery of values.

Bibliography

Achebe, Chinua. 1959. *Things Fall Apart*. New York: Fawcett Crest.
————. 1979. "An Image of Africa." In *Chant of Saints: A Gathering of Afro-American Literature, Art, and Scholarship*. Edited by Michael S. Harper and Robert B. Stepto. Urbana: University of Illinois Press.

Altieri, Charles. 1990. *Canons and Consequences*. Evanston, IL: Northwestern University Press.

Alvis, John. 1993. "Why a Proper Core Curriculum Is Political and Ought Not to Be Politicized. *Intercollegiate Review* 28, no. 2.

Arnheim, Rudolf. 1992. *Toward a Psychology of Art*. New York: McGraw-Hill.

Austen, Jane. 1966. *Pride and Prejudice*. New York: Norton.

Bahktin, Mikhail. 1973. *Problems with Dostoyevsky's Aesthetics*. Translated by R.W. Rostel. Moscow: Ardis.
————. 1981. *The Dialogic Imagination*. Translated by M. Holquist and C. Emerson. Austin: University of Texas Press.

Barthes, Roland. 1975. *The Pleasure of the Text*. New York: Hill and Wang.
————. 1979. "From Work to Text." In *Textual Strategies in Post-Structural Criticism*. Edited by Josue Harari. Ithaca, NY: Cornell University Press.

B.B.C. Music. 1996. London: B.B.C. Worldwide Publishing, spring.

Beardsley, Monroe. 1958. *Aesthetics*. New York: Harcourt Brace and World.

Bernal, Martin. 1987. *Black Athena: The Afrocentric Roots of Classical Civilization.* New Brunswick, NJ: Rutgers University Press.

Bloom, Harold. 1994. *The Western Canon.* New York: Riverhead Books.

Buchler, Justus, ed. 1955. *Writings of Peirce.* New York: Dover Press.

Campbell, SueEllen. 1989. "The Land and the Language of Desire." *Western American Literature* 24, no. 3.

Cassirer, Ernst. 1946. *Language and Myth.* Translated by Susanne Langer. New York: Dover Publications.

Conrad, Joseph. 1971. *Heart of Darkness.* Edited by R. Kimbrough. New York: Norton.

Curtler, Hugh, ed. 1984. *What Is Art?* New York: Haven Publications.

Deleuze, Gilles, and Félix Guattari. 1983. *Anti-Oedipus.* Minneapolis: University of Minnesota Press.

Eaton, Marcia. 1988. *Basic Issues in Aesthetics.* Belmont, CA: Wadsworth Press.

Fairchild, Halford. 1995. "Knowing Black History Isn't Just for Blacks." *Los Angles Times,* February 5.

Foucault, Michel. 1984. *The Foucault Reader.* Edited by Paul Rabinow. New York: Pantheon Books.

Gass, William. 1977. *Fiction and the Figures of Life.* New York: Vintage Books.

Gilbert, Rita. 1992. *Living with Art.* New York: McGraw-Hill.

Goethe, Wolfgang. n.d. *Jubiläums-Ausgabe.* Vol. 38. Stuttgart and Berlin: n.p.

Graf, Gerald. 1992. *Beyond the Culture Wars.* New York: Norton.

Heilbroner, Robert. 1985. *The Nature and Logic of Capitalism.* New York: Norton.

Heller, Erich. 1965. *The Disinherited Mind.* New York: World.

Himmelfarb, Gertrude. 1995. *The De-Moralization of Society.* New York: Knopf.

Hofstadter, Richard. 1965. *The Paranoid Style in American Politics and Other Essays.* New York: Knopf.

Hospers, John. 1982. *Understanding the Arts.* Englewood Cliffs, NJ: Prentice-Hall.

Inge, William. 1920. *The Idea of Progress.* Oxford, U.K.: Oxford University Press.

Jessop, T.E. 1969. "The Definition of Beauty." In *Introductory Readings in Aesthetics.* Edited by John Hospers. New York: Free Press.

Jung, Carl. 1933. *Modern Man in Search of a Soul.* Translated by W.S. Dell and Cary F. Baynes. New York: Harcourt Brace and World.
————. 1961. *Psychological Reflections.* Edited by Jolande Jacobi. New York: Harper and Row.
Kaufman, Walter. 1954. *The Portable Nietzsche.* New York: Viking Press.
Kearney, Richard. 1984. *Dialogues with Contemporary Continental Thinkers.* Manchester, U.K.: Manchester University Press.
Koestler, Arthur. 1964. *The Act of Creation.* New York: Dell.
Köhler, Wolfgang. 1959. *The Place of Value in a World of Fact.* New York: Meridian Books.
————. 1969. *The Task of Gestalt Psychology.* Princeton, NJ: Princeton University Press.
Krutch, Joseph. 1956. *Modern Temper.* New York: Harcourt Brace and World.
Lasch, Christopher. 1991. *The Culture of Narcissism.* New York: Norton.
Lee, Vernon. 1933. *Music and Its Lovers.* New York: Dutton.
Lefkowitz, Mary. 1996. *Not out of Africa.* New York: Basic Books.
Levine, Lawrence. 1996. *The Opening of the American Mind.* Boston: Beacon Press.
Lingis, Alphonso. 1994. *The Community of Those Who Have Nothing in Common.* Bloomington: Indiana University Press.
Lyotard, Jean-François. 1992. *The Postmodern Explained.* Minneapolis: University of Minnesota Press.
Marcuse, Herbert. 1964. *One-Dimensional Man.* Boston: Beacon Press.
Martindale, Colin. 1996. "Empirical Questions Deserve Empirical Answers." *Philosophy and Literature* 20, no. 2 (October).
Megill, Allan. 1985. *Prophets of Extremity.* Berkeley: University of California Press.
Meyer, Leonard. 1967. *Music, the Arts, and Ideas.* Chicago: University of Chicago Press.
Murdoch, Marvin. 1971. "The Originality of Joseph Conrad." In *Heart of Darkness.* Edited by Robert Kimbrough. New York: Norton.
Nehamas, Alexander. 1985. *Nietzsche: Life as Literature.* Cambridge, MA: Harvard University Press.
Newton, Lisa. 1992. "Reverse Discrimination as Unjustified." In *Taking Sides.* Edited by Maureen Ford and Lisa Newton. Guilford, CT: Dushkin.

Nietzsche, Friedrich Wilhelm. 1954. *The Portable Nietzsche*. Edited by Walter Kaufman. New York: Viking Press.

———. *Beyond Good and Evil* (*BGE*). (Any edition; numbers in text refer to sections.)

———. *Birth of Tragedy* (*BT*).

———. *Genealogy of Morals* (*GM*).

———. *Gay Science* (*GS*).

———. *Will to Power* (*WTP*).

Norris, Christopher. 1987. *Derrida*. Cambridge, MA: Harvard University Press.

Ornstein, Robert. 1976. *The Mind Field*. New York: Viking Press.

Ortega y Gasset, José. 1960. *Revolt of the Masses*. New York: Norton.

———. 1961. *Meditations on Quixote*. New York: Norton.

Peirce, Charles. 1934. *Collected Papers*. Vols. 5 and 6. Cambridge, MA: Harvard University Press.

———. 1955. *Philosophical Writings of Peirce*. Edited by Justus Buchler. New York: Dover.

Plutarch. 1992. *The Rise and Fall of Athens*. Translated by Ian Scott-Kilvert. New York: Penguin Books.

Popper, Karl. 1968. *The Logic of Scientific Discovery*. New York: Harper and Row.

Proust, Marcel. 1932. *Remembrance of Things Past*. Translated by Scott Montcrieff. New York: Random House.

Rabinow, Paul, ed. 1984. *Foucault Reader*. New York: Pantheon Books.

Richter, David, ed. 1994. *Falling into Theory*. Boston: Bedford Books.

Rosenau, Pauline Marie. 1992. *Post-Modernism and the Social Sciences*. Princeton, NJ: Princeton University Press.

Schrag, Calvin O. 1992. *The Resources of Rationality*. Bloomington: Indiana University Press.

Smith, Barbara Herrnstein. 1988. *Contingencies of Value*. Cambridge, MA: Harvard University Press.

Steiner, George. 1996. *No Passion Spent*. New Haven, CT: Yale University Press.

Tawney, R.H. 1962. *Religion and the Rise of Capitalism*. Gloucester, MA: Peter Smith.

Tompkins, Jane. 1994. "Masterpiece Theater: The Politics of Hawthorne's Literary Reputation." In *Falling into Theory*. Edited by David Richter. Boston: Bedford Books.

Toynbee, Arnold. 1963. *A Study of History*. Vol. 1. Oxford, U.K.: Oxford University Press.

Tussman, Joseph. 1970. *Obligation and the Body Politic*. Oxford, U.K.: Oxford University Press.

Vivas, Eliseo. 1963. *The Artistic Transaction*. Columbus: Ohio State University Press.

Walzer, Michael. 1994. *Thick and Thin: Moral Argument at Home and Abroad*. Notre Dame, IN: University of Notre Dame Press.

Weinstein, Michael. 1995. *Culture/Flesh*. Lanham, MD: Rowman and Littlefield.

West, Cornell. 1993. *Keeping Faith*. New York: Routledge and Kegan Paul.

Wilcox, Stewart. 1971. "Conrad's Complicated Presentations of Symbolic Imagery." In *Heart of Darkness*. Edited by Robert Kimbrough. New York: Norton.

Wofford, Susan, ed. 1994. *Hamlet*. New York: St. Martin's Press.

Wortham, Anne. 1992. "Errors of the Afrocentrists." *Academic Questions* 5, no. 4.

Zweig, Paul. 1976. *Three Journeys: An Automythology*. New York: Basic Books.

Index

Hugh Mercer Curtler received his B.A. from St. John's College in Annapolis, Maryland, and his M.A. and Ph.D. from Northwestern University. He is currently professor of philosophy at Southwest State University, where he also directs the Honors Program. He has authored or edited seven books, including *Ethical Argument* and *What Is Art?*